T0374445

BLUE-COLLAR
BELIEVER

Chaplain William H. Schnakenberg IV

Foreword by
Apologist James Bishop
and
Chaplain Mike Connolly

WESTBOW
PRESS®
A DIVISION OF THOMAS NELSON
& ZONDERVAN

WestBow Press books may be ordered through booksellers or by contacting:

WestBow Press
A Division of Thomas Nelson & Zondervan
1663 Liberty Drive
Bloomington, IN 47403
www.westbowpress.com
1 (866) 928-1240

ISBN: 978-1-5127-5399-8 (sc)
ISBN: 978-1-5127-5398-1 (e)

Library of Congress Control Number: 2016913768

Print information available on the last page.

WestBow Press rev. date: 08/23/2016

Involuntary ignorance is not charged against you as a fault;
but your fault is this:
you neglect to inquire into the things you are ignorant of.

—Augustine
Christian Theologian, Philosopher
13 November 354–28 August 430

=

CONTENTS

FOREWORD

Though geographic location separates Chaplain Bill and me, I have been hugely blessed to have been able to interact with him. I have come to learn that he is a man who loves both his family and his Lord Jesus immensely. In this way he has been a true role model for me, and I truly believe that he has been an inspiration for others. So I was pleasantly surprised and humbled that he would approach me to supply a brief foreword for his book! It was an opportunity that I could not refuse. I am truly humbled by such a request.

What lies in his piece is a journey of brutal honesty and self-reflection. It is an inspiring personal testimony of how the once spiritually lost may be found in their Lord Jesus Christ. His journey, as any reader will see, is one full of obstacles, struggles, fears, failures, and temptations—things that we are all familiar with whether we're Christ followers or not. But it is also a narrative of perseverance, patience, compassion, and, ultimately, a story of love. What Chaplain Bill has really shown me is how strength and hope may be found in the direst of circumstances that life throws our way. It is within these circumstances (much relating to his own father, his childhood, teenage years, and beyond) that the reader embarks on a journey of his or her own personal self-reflection. As I read through his story I realized just how easy I've had things in comparison to many, many people out there in the world. This is what I believe makes his story a worthy one to interact with; it allows us to put ourselves into his shoes and thus self-reflect; and besides that, everybody loves a good story!

A further point worth mentioning is that he has also shown me that one does not need to be someone famous with a massive following or even someone with an advanced education to have a story that is well worth being told. Certainly not. The truth is that every individual has a story, every story matters, and so within these very pages, you shall be blessed by his.

Apologist James Bishop
Cape Town, South Africa
Visit: James Bishop's Theology & Apologetics

This book you're holding, *Blue-Collar Believer,* which has been written from the heart, mind, and personal life experiences of Chaplain Bill, contains everything that is needed to easily share the Word of God with non-Christians. Chaplain Bill has a burning desire to help equip other believers in Christ with the simple tools necessary to present the Bible to non-Christians. He has dedicated several years seeking God's heart, mind, and will through earnest prayer and the study of the Bible to ensure that even the most ardent skeptics be persuaded to seriously question their reasons for not believing in the existence of God.

Chaplain Bill also believes that by sharing with us many of his personal life stories and experiences, both before and after he received Jesus as his Savior, that we everyday blue-collar believers—those of us without theological degrees or other formal biblical training and education—will, come to readily employ his simple teachings to help us better communicate to those presently without the knowledge of God

For both the hardened atheist and the earnest but skeptical agnostic as well as those seeking the truth as it relates to God, creation, His plan of salvation and eternal life, Chaplain Bill has taken the anxiety out of sharing the gospel with all unbelievers, no matter how educated or uneducated they may be.

Within the pages of *Blue-Collar Believer,* we soon come to discover that sharing our personal faith in God with others (something we may not have believed possible without possessing a college Bible degree) is indeed now more than possible. Thanks be to God for Chaplain Bill and his work within these pages, for now we too can successfully argue with the best skeptical minds not only that God exists, but that He loves those of the world so much that He gave His only Son, Jesus, who He sent to earth to die for our sins.

I believe you will come to relate to Chaplain Bill's personal life testimony, which regularly speaks of the very dysfunctional family he grew up in, but also how God used all of those often unpleasant and even ungodly experiences to mold and shape Chaplain Bill into the godly, loving, and caring family man and minister of the gospel he is today.

May God truly bless and inspire you just as He has me, through the reading of *Blue-Collar Believer*, to do what you have always wanted to do but were afraid to do—to step out in faith and confidence and begin sharing the true and living God and His love with others.

Yours in Christ,
Chaplain Mike Connolly
First Church of the Nazarene
Prescott, Arizona

INTRODUCTION

I do thank you for taking the time to pick up this book; it indeed took a lot of time to put together. Along with many exhausting hours of research, reading, studying, all the notes that I have accumulated throughout the years, putting them together, holding down two jobs, being a husband and a father of two young children (with one on the way as well as I type this), an unexpected life-altering event that happened while I was writing it (which changed the entire direction of where this book was headed), and trying to remember the early years of my life, I never thought I would actually have the time to put it all together; but by God's grace, He finally let me do the two things that I love to do: share the gospel and write about it! You are definitely in for an interesting read!

When I first decided to write this book, I had a certain direction in mind. But then, while typing the second chapter, I underwent a major life change. Some would consider it a "trial" or a period of "testing" of faith, but through much perseverance, prayer, trust, and hope in God, I prevailed and became not only stronger in the faith, but I have also decided to include it in this book. Many people I have talked to said they would have given up the faith altogether during the experience I went through, but I am happy to say that I am stronger now in the faith than I have ever been, and I do hope that this experience and everything that I share with you will only strengthen your faith too. If you are not a believer, then I hope that you will take an honest approach to what you are reading and consider it without a personal bias.

What altered the direction of this book was taking care of my dad, my best friend, while he was on hospice. This experience for me was very trying, because I was his full-time aide for two and a half months, and I slowly watched his health decline until he took his last breath and left this world. It was the most painful but joyful time I ever had with my dad. I will go into more detail on that later in the book.

First and foremost I need to make something crystal clear, and that is I am a Christian. If you need to classify me a type of Christian, then you can consider me a "non-denominational historical evidentialist and fundamentalist."

This is the way that I classify myself, if you need to know.

To me, this means that I adhere to the basic beliefs of early Christianity, which expounds on the historical bodily resurrection of Jesus, or as many would call it, the event.

This is what early Christians professed, believed, proclaimed, and died for knowing it as the truth.

This should be an elementary belief for *all* Christians, regardless of what denomination or church membership they are affiliated with. Everything else is secondary, so I do not need to be classified under a certain Christian denomination or be identified under a religious body with a name, defined by a certain structure, adhere to a strict theology, doctrine, or church authority. I do realize that this may be important to some believers, and I do respect their opinion on the matter, but to me it just is not relevant.

Many people have a different perspective on the meaning of a fundamentalist, which I can agree with as well. The word traditionally refers to:

"Any follower of Christ who believes that the Bible is the inspired Word of God and who believes in its literal interpretation and fundamental teachings." – Dr. Dale A. Robbins (Victorious Christian Ministries)

The fundamental Christian believes in the experience of the new birth, which occurs when faith is placed in Christ as Savior and Lord. I do agree with this as well, because what I am about to disclose in this book is indeed what happened to me. To the world this may seem a bit radical, but it is very basic to the Christian faith.

The idea of Christian fundamentalism goes a step further, as stated at a Bible conference meeting in Niagara in 1895 (The Oxford Dictionary of the Christian Church). A statement was issued containing what came to be known as the five points of fundamentalism

1. The verbal inerrancy of scripture
2. The divinity of Jesus Christ
3. The virgin birth
4. A substitutionary theory of the atonement
5. The physical resurrection and bodily return of Christ

The bottom line is that fundamentalism may be used to describe Christians who are uncompromising and who take their beliefs very seriously. Which is exactly how *every* Christian should live.

I became a Christian on December 8, 2008, which dramatically changed my life. I was thirty-two years old when this happened, so I had a lot of experience being a non-Christian and living the unbelieving life with my own personal moral code, which involved drugs, alcohol, womanizing, and living a very foolish lifestyle.

Becoming a Christian changed my life in such a way with a series of events and experiences that I could not choose to ignore. I knew that my life would never be the same, and the gospel is now what my entire earthly life is about while I am still in this body.

I want to make you aware of a couple of things. I do not have a college education or a seminary degree. The highest level of education that I achieved was twelfth grade, and that was by the skin of my teeth. You may feel moved to judge me and think, *Well, this guy probably does not know what he is talking about, especially with a lack of formal education of religion*, but before you do this, know that doing so means you commit a logical fallacy known as a genetic fallacy, which occurs when a claim is accepted or rejected based on the source of the evidence rather than on the quality or applicability of the evidence. It is also a line of reasoning in which a perceived defect in the origin of a claim is taken to be evidence that discredits the claim itself. The fallacy is committed when an idea is either accepted or rejected because of its source rather than its merit.

This is why I do believe that God has placed on my heart and led me to write this book as an autodidact. It is for my fellow blue-collar believers, for "Sunday Miss-tians" (I'll elaborate on this meaning later on in the book), seekers, and unbelievers who are misinformed or misguided, as well as people who do not have the time to truly dive into research on the subject of defending the faith, or what many people know as apologetics.

Furthering our education is a wonderful thing, don't get me wrong; but many of us just were not presented with the opportunity due to financial constraints or other factors and joined the workforce right after high school. Then basically the busyness of life happens.

Does this mean that all blue-collar believers are weak and simple-minded fools who are following a blind faith?

That would be a negative. Some maybe are, but to say *all* is wrong.

The Christian faith goes beyond what many people would look at as a blind faith. People who believe this are the ones who are blind as well as ignorant.

That would be affirmative.

Now your mouth may have dropped by reading such a word, and you may not believe that I have said it, but I will say it again—*ignorant.*

Living in a politically correct society, how could I say such a thing?

It is because I am not afraid to boldly speak up for and defend the Christian faith, and I am not worried about agreeing with the idea that people should be careful to not use language or behave in a way that could offend a particular group of people over religious beliefs. Religion is not a personal matter, regardless of what many people may think. The gospel is a message that *needs* to be shared, it can and should be defended, and it is the decision of the individual who it is being shared with to either accept or reject it.

Most people do not even understand what the word *ignorance* means.

Ignorance basically means having or showing a" lack of knowledge or information on a subject."

Many of the people that I have encountered presenting, sharing, and talking about the gospel sure do show it;

believers and unbelievers alike. It does not matter how educated you think you are. You may have all kinds of certificates and diplomas hanging on your wall from a secular institution, but the fact of the matter is that these are only pieces of paper. They do not make you who you are. Christians are who we are in Christ, with or without a higher education, and God grants godly wisdom to all those who are honestly seeking Him.

But seek ye first the kingdom of God, and His righteousness; and all these things shall be added unto you.—Matthew 6:33

We usually acquire this through life experiences; things we cannot learn in a school setting. I would rather have godly wisdom than worldly wisdom because I am who I am because of Him. I do not need to be a worldly intellectual to know this.

Now is ignorance such a bad thing?

I can admit that I am ignorant of many things. I do not have all the answers about everything, but when it comes to spiritual or religious beliefs I am ready to argue points that now I have come to realize many people are ignorant about. I was there, so I can completely empathize with many people as you will come to learn reading this book.

To argue does not mean to have a fist fight and a yelling match, although sadly many arguments do lead to this type of ungodly behavior. A true argument is to persuade someone by giving reasons, or to give reasons for or against something.

If this can be done with good, rational, and well thought out reasons without personal bias in a gentle, courteous manner, listening to one another, without attacking someone's character, sticking to the subject, and avoiding logical fallacies, then an argument can be a wonderful thing. We can actually overcome ignorance by understanding one another through an argument.

No one can force beliefs on anyone. If we have learned anything from the ugliness in history, the rise of political power, and human greed within and without the Christian community, this is a fact. Even Christopher Columbus when he landed in America, after meeting the first natives, recorded in one of his many personal journal entries the following account, "though his heart was to be well-disposed towards the natives, because he knew that they were a people to be delivered and converted to the Gospel rather by love than by force," – *American Journeys Collection, Journal of the first voyage of Columbus, document No. AJ-062, Wisconsin Historical Society Digital Library and Archives 2003*

This is where he went wrong with his thinking. Force should *never* be an option.

With proper argumentation, people can rise above ignorance, and if the Lord is willing, become persuaded by the truth. The bottom line is that it is a choice—the gospel is a message to be accepted or rejected.

Let me talk about the design on the cover of the book. You will notice that the words "blue-collar believer" are strategically placed inside the design of a blue collar. Blue collar is defined as a working class male or female who has a paying job doing manual labor.

Not many people may realize this, but Jesus Himself was in fact a woodworker by trade in His day, or nowadays people may refer to Him as a carpenter. His specialty most likely was to make doors or furniture for stone or mud-brick houses as well as plows and yokes for farmers. As a craftsman He could be compared to a blue-collar worker in the current generation in lower-middle-class America. So if you are a blue-collar believer, what better role model could you possibly have than Jesus?

Historically, the term *blue collar* comes from the industrial and manual workers who would often wear clothing that may get dirty during the course of their work. Navy and light-blue colors do a better job concealing potential dirt or grease on the workers' clothing, helping it to appear cleaner. A higher level academic education is often not required for many blue-collar jobs.

Nowadays blue-collar jobs may involve being skilled in a type of physical work, which can take place in or out of an office environment. It is considered possibly lower level in pay and may also involve sitting at a computer or desk at times, but manual labor is still part of the job description.

You will also notice on the cover design a shield with the bottom of a boot footprint on it. This is a metaphor for the working class because many blue-collar workers need to wear steel toe boots to protect their feet from a painful mishap or accident.

The shield is a metaphor for *defend*, and this is where the gospel defense comes into play. We must always keep in mind that a shield can be used as a weapon for offense as well. People seem to think a shield is only for defense, but it can turn into a mighty offensive weapon that can put down an attack.

Blue-collar workers are people who keep the world moving. Without them the economy would be in ruins. The world needs and depends on them more than you think. It is not a position that should be frowned on, although many white-collar workers may do so. Hold your head up high and be proud of what you do regardless of what you do! Whether you clean a toilet, deliver mail, drive a truck, dig ditches, or generally get your hands dirty on the job, an honest day of work to pay your bills and feed your family surpasses any illegal activity to make money, and you can go to sleep each night with a clear conscience.

Does that sound like something to take lightly?

Ask the common street thug who has to look over his shoulder wherever he goes and cannot sleep at night because he's worried that he may be killed. It is a lifestyle that has more cons than pros, and money is not everything.

Blue-collar workers work hard, long hours; they often must work unannounced mandatory overtime; operate in very stressful situations; don't make much money; are often forced to take pay cuts, are not recognized for a job well done by employers; and do not have much time to devote to ourselves, our families, and more importantly, our faith.

We interact with many different types of religious and non-religious people in and out of the workforce on a daily basis, and the Christian faith is often viewed in a negative way. This happens for a variety of reasons, and many people want to speak up to defend the faith when confronted but are afraid to, or just do not know how to. They may also fear confrontation or feel that they are not equipped to defend the faith, and this needs to be addressed.

But how do we speak up boldly for the faith, confident that we have the answers to possible criticism from skeptics?

Since we are a working-class type of people, you may be able to identify with me a lot better than you would an expert in the field of apologetics or a theologian. Also, sometimes pastors or elders of churches are not equipped in the study of apologetics or sometimes don't even think it is important. This saddens me very much. Don't get me wrong—there is a lot of help out there if you are willing to make the commitment, but many of us are just not able to devote the time. In a like manner, words and types of arguments can get quite tricky and hard to understand if you have not done proper research.

This is the entire point of this book: to help you learn how to defend the faith in a simple, blue-collar way. This book is designed to be read rather quickly, and it's written by a blue-collar believer for a blue-collar believer because if I can do it, anyone can. Although I do hope reading this book may spark a curiosity in you to learn more about Christian apologetics. There is a wealth of information out there, and I am not going to get too deep into all the fantastic attributes apologetics can bring to help you strengthen your faith. Research the subject yourself as it is quite fascinating.

There are a variety of types of arguments that are modern but oftentimes disguised with a new twist. However, they are in fact the same old arguments that have been around for centuries and have been well refuted. Scholarly Christian apologists adapt to most of them or specialize in a certain area and are ready to defend the view.

Here are some types of arguments followed by a brief explanation that are very common. I've listed them in alphabetical order except for the last four because those topics I address most in the book. Most of the arguments are philosophical, which in a nutshell means they defend the position of "the rational investigation of certain truths and principles of being, knowledge, or conduct."-*Dictionary.com*

Sample Apologetics Arguments:

Biblical: defends the position of biblical inerrancy (the Bible being free from error).

Cosmological: defends the position that the universe requires an external cause (God).

Creation: defends the position along with the cosmological argument including theories of young earth (10,000 years or younger) or an old earth (10,001-plus years or more).

Ontological: defends the position that the very concept of God demands that there is an actual existent God, which gets into metaphysics (a study of what is outside objective experience, or based on facts rather than feelings or opinions) concerned with the nature and relations of being.

Presuppositional: defends the position that the Christian faith is the only basis for rational thought and that there are no neutral assumptions from which a Christian can reason with a non-Christian.

Scientific: defends the position that science and the Bible do not contradict each other.

Teleological (fine tuning): defends the position that there is a purposeful design in the world and that the design requires a designer.

Transcendental: defends the position that our abilities to think and reason require the existence of God.

Prophetic: defends the position that there are many Old Testament prophecies (explicit predictions about the future sometimes hundreds or even thousands of years apart) fulfilled by Jesus in the New Testament. (This argument led my dad to Christ.)

Moral: defends the position that real moral obligation is a fact, and if there are any real objectively valid moral values, there must be an absolute from which they are derived. (This argument led me to Christ.)

Experiential, Religious Experience, or Testimony: defends the position primarily that a self-verifying experience is evidence for the Christian faith. This view stresses experience that other Christians may not have experienced in the same way, but the concept that the Holy Spirit and/or conscience convinces the heart of truth is always the central theme.

Historical evidentialist: defends the position using the historicity of the bodily resurrection of Christ. (This argument has not only helped me grow as a Christian but has enhanced my faith in Christ.)

Do these arguments seem a bit overwhelming?

Did you know about them?

All of these arguments listed are great arguments, but I feel the Lord has especially enlightened me on the last four, which allows me to share the gospel and see unbelievers be persuaded and respond in a positive way. Though we must always keep in mind that it is the Holy Spirit that enlightens the individual; all we do is plant the seed. God makes the seed grow.

This by no means is an exhaustive list of arguments; they are just some that I have looked into during my years as a Christian. Some of them may seem a bit complex, which is completely understandable, but you do not have to know about all of them to have a valid argument and feel confident to defend the faith.

The reason we need to understand arguments such as these is so we can defend the faith when we come into contact with someone says things like, "Well, I don't believe the Bible is the word of God," or "God does not exist," or "Jesus was just a myth—I believe in evolution and not creation," and so on.

It is *how* we argue that is of the upmost importance.

But sanctify the Lord God in your hearts: and *be ready always to give an answer to every man that asketh you a reason* of the hope that is in you with meekness and fear: Having a good conscience; that, whereas they speak evil of you, as of evildoers, they may be ashamed that falsely accuse your good conversation in Christ (italics mine).—1 Peter 3:15–16

Casting down (*destroying*) imaginations (*arguments*), and every high thing that exalteth itself against the knowledge of God, and bringing into captivity every thought to the obedience of Christ.—2 Corinthians 10:5

The fact of the matter is that we all need to know the basics, which a lot of us already do, but we just do not know how to put what we already know into words. This is what I hope to help you with in this book and especially with my experiences.

All scripture that I use in this book will be referenced from the (KJV), otherwise known as the King James Version. I do prefer the King James Version for many reasons, but I also hold most Bible translations in the highest regard because they do their best to translate correctly.

What we must keep in mind is that most biblical scholars hold that the New Testament (Matthew-Revelation) was written over 1,900 years ago in Greek. The Old Testament (Genesis-Malachi) was written in Hebrew much earlier than that, possibly the earliest writings were written around 1,400 BC. They then were translated to Greek and then to English. From this view point of language, a perfect translation can't be made from Greek to English or especially from Hebrew to Greek and then to English. There is lots of room for error and word play. Interpretations can vary a little or a lot, and often there are not even words that can translate from Greek to English, but translators do their best when they come across these instances.

There are three translations that virtually all scholars have found to have been purposefully altered by leaders to meet an organization's false beliefs and teachings. Their followers/members genuinely believe their organization holds to the truth, but they are following a false teaching:

- New World Translation (NWT)
  - Jehovah's Witnesses use this version.

- Joseph Smith Translation (JST) or Inspired Version (IV)
  - The Church of Jesus Christ of Latter-day Saints/Mormons use this version.

- The Queen James Bible (QJB)

- "Some" supporters of the Lesbian Gay Bisexual Transgender (LGBT) community use this version.

So if you are still with me, I am going to begin the book with my life before becoming a Christian.

CHAPTER 1

My Life as an Unbeliever

The acquaintances, friends, companions, family, and people in general who I have met and had in my life before I was a Christian know me best in the way I am going to describe in this chapter; however, many of the people I know now living as a Christian do not know the details that I am about to disclose in this chapter.

Some of the people who know me now may be shocked and appalled about what they are about to read. As embarrassing as some of the information I am going to share may be for me, I do believe in my heart that it needs to be shared. The fact of the matter is that I am not proud of the lifestyle I lived before becoming a Christian, but it is important to know where I came from because every Christian has a past. Their conversions are a product of something beautiful, and there are lives that they left behind.

Take a look at "Saul," better known as Paul, who most likely wrote or dictated thirteen of the letters in the New

Testament; additionally, he is the subject of most of the book of Acts.

Here are four quick examples of what he was like prior to his conversion:

And Saul, yet breathing out threatenings and slaughter against the disciples of the Lord, went unto the high priest, And desired of him letters to Damascus to the synagogues, that if he found any of this way, whether they were men or women, he might bring them bound unto Jerusalem. (Acts 9:1-2)

"This way" meaning followers of Christ. This was an early description of who Christians were.

For I am the least of the apostles, that am not meet to be called an apostle, because I persecuted the church of God. (1 Corinthians 15:9)

He persecuted Christians.

And they stoned Stephen, calling upon God, and saying, Lord Jesus, receive my spirit. And he kneeled down, and cried with a loud voice, Lord, lay not this sin to their charge. And when he had said this, he fell asleep. (Acts 7:59-60)

And Saul was consenting unto his death. And at that time there was a great persecution against the church. (Acts 8:1)

He consented to the death of the first Christian martyr Stephen.

I think you get the picture that Paul was not an advocate for Christianity in any way prior to his conversion. The reality is that Christians become Christians because we are *far* from being perfect. We all have a past. If anyone tells you differently, they are telling and/or living a lie. We all had a past life before we heard and responded to the gospel; some former lives may be more painful or unpleasant than others, but we all have a story we lived that should be shared.

Therefore, if anyone is in Christ, he is a new creation; old things have passed away; behold, all things have become new. (2 Corinthians 5:17)

I have lost many friends because of my current Christian beliefs, not because I tried to push religion on them but because my views on life in general have changed. I have attained a Christian worldview, and to many people this is just not acceptable. I have gained many more brothers and sisters in Christ, and as for the friends who have stayed with me after my conversion, I am proud to say most of them are now Christians too.

So let me begin with a little background on my life. I was born on July 19, 1976, on Long Island, New York. I was baptized shortly thereafter in Saint Patrick's Roman Catholic Church in the town of Huntington. My mother, father, my teenage half-sister (my godmother), and my great uncle (my godfather) were all present according to the baptism certificate that I found in my dad's safety deposit box.

My mother was brought up as a Roman Catholic and attended Catholic school from her childhood through adolescence.

She ended up leaving the RCC and is now a Lutheran. My father, on the other hand, went to a Methodist church when he was a young boy; after that, the Christian faith and religion in general were not really important to him.

A year later my sister was born; they called us Irish twins because we are the same age for five days each year.

I don't really remember much about my early childhood, just a wooded area behind our yellow house that I loved to explore and a great big hill in the front of the house that was great for sledding. I recall that when my grandmother was visiting from Florida and she wanted me to stay out of the woods she told me that a great big lizard escaped from the zoo and was hiding in the woods ready to eat little children (talk about striking a fear into a child!). She also used to use a tube of lipstick to draw a target in the toilet so I had somewhere to visibly aim. I think that my wife may want to do this with me now!

I remember random things like sliding down the stairs in a sleeping bag and a particular Christmas when I got a cardboard rocket ship that I thought was the greatest gift in the world. *Star Wars* was a big movie back then, and I remember having a *Star Wars*–themed birthday party.

I am reminded that when I went to kindergarten, it was the first time I had ever seen a child-size urinal. When I first saw it, someone had used it as it was not intended to be used, and that was how I thought it was supposed to be used. I proceeded to use the urinal to do my "wrong business" for many months until a teacher caught me doing so. She

4

explained to me that a urinal was only to be used for number one and not number two, and so began my corrected potty breaks. How embarrassing!

In 1983, when I was seven years old, I became a big brother again to another little sister. We then moved to Centerport, Long Island. I loved our new house and have many fond memories of living there. I think this is where I had my first official girlfriend. She was a little German girl from school. She passed me a note in class, and it said, "Do you like me? Check yes or no." I checked yes, and we were in a secret official relationship. Due to reasons I am not sure of, the relationship did not last too long, and I hope it was not because she found out about the number two urinal issue!

This was the time in life when I looked forward to Saturday morning: cartoons and WWF with Hulk Hogan, Roddy Piper, and Jimmy "Superfly" Snuka; eating Lucky Charms or Cocoa Pebbles for breakfast; playing with He-man, GI-Joe, or the original *Star Wars* action figures.

I was an admirer of Alex P. Keaton (Michael J. Fox) from the sitcom *Family Ties* and would even dress like him in a suit and tie and go to public school sometimes wearing this attire. I would carry around a Bible, not that I read or understood what it meant, but maybe this was a sign of things to come later in my life? My mother even thought that I would be a pastor someday. How interesting°…

There was no such thing as time-outs in those days—we were disciplined by a smack with a wooden spoon by Mom, and if it was something really bad, she often said, "Wait until your father gets home!" We lived on a big pond, had a rowboat, and winters were awesome for ice skating. I made many friends there, was involved in Cub Scouts, baseball, and soccer; happily, I was a very active young boy.

This is the first time I have any recollection of attending church. I don't really remember much about the church, but I remember being involved in Christmas plays and Cub Scouts Pinewood Derbies, which were held there: One time my dad and I even won, and it was the greatest.

My friends and I would ride our bikes to the dam and fish, which meant catching flounder and throwing them back. I remember getting worms at a local snack shop, along with a Yoo-hoo and some candy. The highlight of these years was when my dad took me and a friend—gloves in tow, in the hope of catching a foul ball—to a New York Mets game at Shea Stadium. Oh, the 1980s: Dwight Gooden, Mookie Wilson, Daryl Strawberry, Lenny Dykstra, and the greatest catcher that ever lived—Gary Carter. They were all my heroes of the era! I was ten years old when they won the World Series in 1986, and it was a day I will never forget. That same year, the New York Giants, my favorite football team, won their first Super Bowl.

In 1987, when I was eleven years old, my father landed a job in Princeton, New Jersey, and we moved to Pennsylvania. I was really heartbroken to leave New York; I thought that being in Pennsylvania was like living down south: I was going to turn into a redneck hillbilly living in "Pensly-tucky."

The move was an adjustment for everyone, but we adapted well. Our new home was a beautiful; it had a secret stairway in the closet and a huge barn on the property. The previous owner of the house was Mr. Rogers' sister. Yes, the Mr. Rogers of the show famous for the phrase Welcome to my neighborhood" with Mr. McFeely, the crazy and fast mailman.

In a town called Souderton, we began to attend a Brethren in Christ Church, which lasted until 1992. By no means were we a religious family. I mean, we said grace before dinner, but that is all I can remember about God being brought up at home, unless of course His name was used as a curse word. We all dreaded going to church on Sundays, but my mom made us. She was always very active in the church and liked getting involved. I remember my dad sleeping through the sermons, my mom nudging him to wake up, and my sisters and I not listening and just playing around.

I would say that I had a pretty normal childhood up until my parents' divorce in April 1992. It was a surprise to all of us, except my mom. We all were called to the kitchen table, and Mom basically said that she and my dad were getting a divorce because she was "not happy." My sister immediately slammed her fist on the table and yelled, "I will never leave my daddy!"

The news devastated my family, but most of all my dad. He was heartbroken because he did not want a divorce, and I don't think he ever really recovered from it. In fact, he went into a deep depression, especially when the children were given the option of who they wanted to live with and both of my sisters chose my mother. I had this nightmarish feeling that he would have committed suicide if I had chosen my mom too. This feeling became a reality for me as a sixteen-year-old boy when I had to plead with my father to take his finger off the trigger and withdraw the loaded gun from his mouth. He figured that was the only remedy for the pain that he was experiencing from being alone. After many minutes of tears, I finally convinced him to put the gun down, that I would never leave him, and that he would never be alone. Through the years my dad and I became very close, and he became more of a friend to me than a father in a very strange way.

During this time in my life, I met a girl who I fell in love with at first sight. She was a year younger than me and friends with my sister. She did not like me at first, but with some persuasion, she decided to go out with me. I loved her dearly, and she really helped me with the problems I was having as she was a product of divorce as well. We were from two different worlds though. She was the good girl, and I was the bad boy. But opposites attract, and we were each other's first and I am proud to say last and only true loves.

I think with the stress of not having his family together anymore, my dad really hit rock bottom. He had a minor stroke, and I honestly believe that the stress of the divorce caused the major health issues that plagued my dad for the rest of his life. He began to smoke close to three packs of cigarettes a day and drink more.

During this transition, church life for me completely stopped. My life took a drastic turn, and I became a very rebellious child. My dad worked the third shift, so he slept all day and worked all night. I was very independent and had a lot of freedom. Being a teenage boy in this situation tempted me, and I made some very unwise choices. I started to get into trouble at school, I spent most of my time in detention, and my grades began to plummet. I was then introduced to cigarettes, alcohol, and drugs.

The upside to my new lifestyle now was that my dad worked third shift, so I had the house to myself at night and was able to invite friends over whenever I wanted. My dad and I lived on Hungry Man microwavable meals and hardly saw each other except for the weekends. During his absence I had complete freedom, and hitting up his liquor cabinet became very common, as did liquor being bought by friends' brothers or friends who were twenty-one years or older. Alcohol was always easily accessible, and oh how I loved to drink! I just loved the feeling of being intoxicated. Being drunk made me do things that I would never be able to do while I was sober.

I got in trouble one day at school because a friend of mine and I liked to get drunk before school. We did this about once a week, and I finally got busted because the gym teacher smelled alcohol on me. I ended up getting an out-of-school suspension, and my dad was mad that I hadn't told them that I wore one of his shirts that he spilled booze on the night before. That was my dad—always looking out for me. Whether it was in my best interests or not, he always supported me.

As my teenage years unfolded, not only did I continue to drink, but I began to smoke marijuana as well. Smoking weed and drinking alcohol were very common within the teenage culture where I grew up, and I indulged whenever I could as most curious, rebellious, and defiant teenagers did.

Eventually, my dad sold the house, and we moved in with his cousin who lived a couple of towns away. My dad started dating a woman that he knew from a long time ago. They decided to buy a house together a little farther away, and I moved in with them.

After graduating high school, barely passing with a D average and having to go to summer school, I landed a job as a dishwasher for a fast food company. I worked there for a while with no plan for my life. While most of my other friends went off to college, I lived in the moment partying when I could. I finally came to the realization that I was working a dead-end job and really needed to focus on my future.

I decided to follow in my dad's footsteps and enlisted in the Marine Corps. It is important to note that you have to take and pass physical and written tests before you can even go to boot camp. I was not the brightest intellectual, and it took me three times to pass the written test. The job categories that I could choose from were not scholarly jobs by any means, but my whole goal in joining the Marine Corps was to make a career on the USMC boxing team. I dabbled a lot on my own with mixed martial arts and boxing, and I thought that once I made the team, I wouldn't have to do the job I enlisted for because of training and fights. At the time, that was my heart's desire. So I chose the job of cook with no intention of ever preparing and cooking food or working in a mess hall.

Becoming a Marine broke my (paternal) grandfather's heart because he wanted me to enlist in the army, where he had worked his way up to chief warrant officer. I also broke my (maternal) grandfather's heart because he was in the navy. I often joked with him, saying, "The Marine Corps is part of the navy; you know—the men's department."

In boot camp, I learned a lot about myself, discipline, becoming a Marine, and most importantly, how to be a leader. It was by no means an easy experience, and there were many who did not get through it. In fact, a kid in my platoon tried to commit suicide by drinking a bottle of Drano. I have to admit it was the hardest three months, both mentally and physically, I have ever endured in my life. Clearly, the thing that kept me going was looking forward to seeing my family, especially my dad, on Parris Island watching me graduate: my ultimate proudest moment.

We all exchanged letters by mail, but nothing meant more to me than getting a letter from my dad. He knew exactly what I was going through in each week and phase, and he kept motivating me. I looked forward to each and every letter.

When graduation day finally came, I looked across the great crowds of people and finally zeroed in on my family, but the one person I did not see was my dad. I was sure he drove down with his uncle and my girlfriend. I discovered he apparently had a little too much to drink the night before, had a hangover, and overslept in the hotel room.

My uncle and my girlfriend did their best to get him up so he would not miss the graduation, but he was just too drunk. Though I was beyond disappointed that he did not see me receive the Eagle, Globe, and Anchor and be called a United States Marine, deep down I understood why°…

He saw my sisters and mother together, but they were not *his* family anymore, and he clearly could not handle that. We had a long talk about it, which actually formed a special bond between us, so I understood and forgave him. I know that he was deeply hurt by his actions, but that is something that he had to live with. I still achieved a status that many dreamed of doing and many failed to do, and I had done it with my own blood, sweat, and tears. I was a Marine, and I knew wholeheartedly that he was proud of me, and that is all that counted. He bought me a beautiful graduation present—a white gold Marine Corps ring that I treasured with all of my heart. I valued that ring so much; I just never wanted to take it off.

But after graduating boot camp, it was the same old thing, back to partying and drinking, only *a lot more*. After a week of leave, I had to go to Camp Lejeune in North Carolina for further training. My high school sweetheart went off to college; we got engaged but then called it off and went our separate ways. I truly loved her with all of my heart and knew that I would never love someone like that again.

I got hurt in training, worked on the base in the mailroom, ended up being diagnosed with tendonitis in both feet and then was medically discharged as a lance corporal with a service connected disability. With no choice on where to go next, I moved back in with my dad and his girlfriend.

My younger sister was now in high school and had moved back in with my dad, which made him very happy. However, there were issues because my dad's girlfriend and my sister did not get along.

I landed a job at a supermarket in the seafood department and worked there for a while. Then my dad, looking out for his son like he always does, said he could get me an internship for the summer in the mailroom with the company for which he worked. I was familiar with the mail industry, having worked in one during my rehab in the Marines. In fact, I was there so long and my gunnery sergeant liked me so much that he was trying to get my Military Occupation Schooling changed from cook to mail operations. Thinking the internship would only be temporary, I went for it and got a taste of what the corporate world was like working as a blue-collar worker.

I never stopped partying and lived weekend to weekend. I recall being at a party and getting very, very drunk: All I remember is waking up with a fat lip. Two random girls were trying to clean me up°... that was the first and last time I was ever knocked out. So I drove home, and when I got there discovered I had lost my house key. I knew that if I was both careful and quiet, I could climb onto the roof and through the attic window and then tiptoe to my room.

13

Apparently, I was not quiet enough when I opened the window and jumped in because lo and behold, there stood my dad *in his underwear* pointing a gun and clearly ready to shoot.

There I was, drunk, visibly beaten up from a physical altercation, and almost shot by my own father. It was a night for the books!

I kept my partying under control during the week and still had a sense of responsibility at work. I rarely called out, never came in late, and got along with everyone on the job.

My supervisor and I became really good friends, often hanging out outside of work. As my skills developed, I was promoted to a lead position. I enjoyed what I did, and my supervisor/buddy was a great mentor. I got on the job training and eventually had to begin holding meetings with the work crew. I was scared to death to speak in public, and there was not one time before I held a meeting that I was not nervous about doing so.

Shortly thereafter my sister got into an argument with my dad's girlfriend, packed up her things, and left to go back to live with my mother. My dad was crushed once again. While I was at work I received a call from his girlfriend, who frantically told me that my dad locked himself in the bedroom, was drunk, had a gun, and was going to commit suicide. She said that she was going to call the police. I did my best to calm her down, told her not to call the police, and I immediately left work and went home.

I walked up the stairs to his bedroom and turned the knob, but the door was locked. I pleaded with my dad to open the door, but he said it was over and he could not take anymore. After much persistence, he finally opened the door to a sight I will never forget.

There was my dad, sitting in a chair in the dark, hammered, his handgun loaded, the barrel in his mouth. It was a scene I was all too familiar with, as I had seen it once before. I immediately dropped to my knees and begged him to put the gun down. I cried many tears and pleaded with him. In his intoxicated state he was not very coherent, but he began to listen to me as the only voice of reason. Clearly, I did not know the right things to say in a situation like this because I was not a counselor. Through my tears I tried to reason with him that it was not right for a son to watch his father take his own life—it would create an infernal image that no son should have imprinted in his mind for the rest of his life. Finally, he put the gun on the floor, and he promised would never put me in that position again.

The one thing about my dad was that he was a man of his word. If he made a promise, which he rarely did, he would keep it. Whether he was drunk or not, I knew that I could count on him to never resort to that again.

When I turned twenty-one, a whole new world opened up for me: the bar scene, my dream come true. I was a very outgoing, sociable, and friendly guy, so mixing my personality in a legal drinking atmosphere was absolute heaven.

My friends and I were notorious for standing outside a bar in the morning, waiting for it to open, and then actually being there all day until it closed. It was kind of funny to watch the bartenders change shifts, sometimes twice, right in front of our eyes. My friends and I were not just friends but comrades, and we called each other brothers. They had my back, and I certainly had theirs. Under any circumstance we were there for each other. Not only did we drink, we began to use cocaine very heavily. It was very common for my crew and I to be in a dirty, dingy bar, walk to a foul restroom, and then use the top of an unclean toilet to do drugs. What did we care? We were drunk and high. The last thing we were concerned with was good hygiene.

I drove drunk regularly and often did not remember how I got home. I finally got a DUI, and when I blew the breathalyzer it was twice over the legal limit. I lost my license for six months, had to pay hefty fines, pay my lawyer, and pay to take some DUI courses. Luckily, my supervisor lived near me and gave me a ride to work for six months. Without him, I would have lost my job.

It was a long six months, and when I finally got my license back, it was the same old thing. I was notorious for driving around with a beer in my lap; some people just do not learn. Time went on, and one day I decided to quit my job and move in with some friends who had a house. It was like living in a fraternity house without going to college! I got a job at Walmart, worked third shift, and the partying increased. Not just partying, but now womanizing was at the top of my list because I had a house to bring girls back to without worrying about my dad, his girlfriend, or my little sister interrupting. It was like a dream come true.

Every once in a while my friends and I would head down to the shore. On one particular occasion, we took a trip to Sea Isle City, New Jersey. It was a late night of partying, and I was in the shore house in my bare feet. I stepped outside because I heard some commotion, and there was my good friend standing up against a wall with his girl next to him. In front of them there were a group of about ten guys mouthing off to them. My friend was as drunk as a skunk and holding a beer. As soon as he looked up and saw me, he did the most idiotic thing you could imagine when you are outnumbered: he wound up and threw his beer at one of the guys! It hit him in the face, and he immediately went down.

This is when the chaos and violence began—the nine other guys bum-rushed my friend. When you see your friend outnumbered and hurt, something happens within your soul and your adrenaline takes over. I don't know whether it was my adrenaline or my fighting skills that night (or maybe a combination of both), but I did not get hurt and my friend and I came out of the madness victorious.

We heard sirens in the background and everyone scattered. As my friend and I looked back on this experience years later, we often joked about it, but we were blessed that we were not seriously hurt or even killed. I think that as you get older and look back on certain experiences in your life, you tend to look at them realistically and know that things could have been a lot worse.

My friends and I once took a road trip to Boston for a St. Patrick's Day weekend. We booked a hotel for three nights, and our all-time favorite punk band was playing. We were so excited and were up for a great and unforgettable time.

After the concert the first night we were there, we went bar-hopping to the most well-known bars in the city. All I remember is waking up in a random hotel room on the floor all alone.

I thought to myself, *Where is everybody?* This was the day and age before cell phones were invented, so calling someone was out of the question. I looked at the clock on the wall and it was 10:00 AM. The room did not seem at all familiar to me; I had a massive hangover, my head was pounding, and I could not remember anything from the night prior. None of my friends' bags were on the floor, and I was not in the room I had checked in to.

I thought to myself, *Where am I?*

I frantically checked my pocket looking for my wallet and found it. I opened it up, and I had thirteen dollars. This was a really bad situation because before I left Pennsylvania, I had made a withdrawal at an ATM of close to a thousand dollars!

How could I spend close to a grand in one night?

I could not have gotten robbed—why would they leave me thirteen dollars? Plus, I was not beat up, or was I?

I ran into the bathroom to see if I had any cuts, bruises, or lacerations on my face because I was not hurting anywhere physically except for the massive hangover.

I looked into the mirror and saw that I was fine.

I remembered the number of the room we originally checked in to, so I went out into the hallway to see what the number of this room was.

I was astounded to see that the number on the room that I was in was the same number of the hotel room that my friends and I checked into the day before, but clearly it was not the same hotel.

How was this even possible? What was going on?

I felt like I was in the twilight zone or being punked by Ashton Kutcher!

I walked down to the hotel lobby and spoke with the receptionist at the desk. After an embarrassing and awkward conversation, I learned that I had checked into this hotel the night prior. I was also no longer in Boston, but in a town called Cambridge, which was about a twenty-dollar cab ride back to Boston.

I checked out of the hotel, called a cab, and got a ride back to Boston. I nervously explained the situation to the cab driver, and he thought that it was one of the funniest stories he had ever heard. Although I only had thirteen dollars to give him and the cab toll was twenty-seven dollars, he said not to worry about and actually thanked me for the laugh.

After the cab had dropped me off at the right hotel, in the correct city, and I walked into my real room, my friends came running up to me to find out where I had been. I told them what had happened, and they sure got a laugh out of it. They said the last thing they remembered about me from the night before was being at a bar; I was talking to a girl and then I just disappeared.

For the rest of the weekend, my one friend spotted me money so I could party with the rest of them, and we sure had a blast. It was a weekend to remember, at least the parts I *can* remember!

My friends and I lived moment to moment and pursued women like it was a game. It was like a contest to see who could get the most phone numbers in one night while doing our best to go home with a girl. I have had many nights that I cannot remember, and many mornings I've woken up in a strange bed with a woman I had hooked up with the night before. Waking up somewhere and not remembering how I got there came with the lifestyle.

Alcohol fueled me to go beyond and transcend myself. While intoxicated I did things I would never do while sober. A typical night would start with a couple of shots of Jameson and a six-pack, which made me more confident, more comical, and more desirable. Curiously, I often had this uncanny desire to dance, which never in my right mind would I do. I also had "beer muscles" and therefore no problem whatsoever starting a fight with a guy twice my size. Booze transcended me beyond reality.

I had no problem talking with women either. I'd just buy a girl a drink, and next thing you know I was having an intimate conversation with a really attractive woman—married or single, it did not matter. As I look back, I find it very disturbing; as I am sure you do as well. There were times when I had to hide underneath a bed or sneak out the back door because a husband came home. It was just part of the game. It deeply saddens me that I sunk to this level, not just because of peer pressure, but to fulfil my sexual desires and fantasies, too.

My drugs of choice now were kicked up a notch when I added nitrous oxide, magic mushrooms, acid, and pain pills. Using acid kept me up for several long days and nights of pretty intense parting. When I ran out of cocaine I really felt like a hardcore addict because I would actually crawl along the carpeted floor trying to find chunks of the drug that had either fallen when I cut it, or more disgustingly, dropped out of someone's nose. If I was lucky I would find some, form it into lines, and get one last snort. Occasionally I found a rock or two, more often merely a piece of fuzz; no matter what, it still went up my nose.

I then got fired from my job at Walmart, and to please my parents I voluntarily checked myself into an alcohol rehab center. After recovery I moved in with my mom and got a job working at a nursing home in the kitchen. The rehab place did not work for me, and I was soon back to my old lifestyle.

I got tired of that job because it did not pay much money. I contacted my old boss in the corporate mail center, and he hired me back on good faith. I moved back in with my dad and figured the career change back to the corporate world would help me with my lifestyle. My father and I now worked at the same site, so we also saw each other daily at work. We were very close and had a great relationship. We loved to get together for New York Giants games, which became a tradition with him and me and my sisters every football season. We had already seen the Giants win two Super Bowls together, once in 1986 when I was ten years old and then again in 1990 when I was fourteen years old.

I ended up still partying on weekends and was able to save up enough money to get an apartment with a friend of mine; we had some crazy times together to say the least. We loved when we got our tax return checks back because if we put our money together, we could spend it on one day at a gentleman's club. I was excelling at my job once again and became a supervisor making pretty good money for a guy with no college degree.

I remember September 11, 2001: my dad called me internally on the phone and said to come over with my boss (my good friend) to his office as soon as we could. I stopped what I was doing, grabbed my boss, and we ran through the long, narrow hallway to his office. He had a television, it was on, and all three of us watched in horror as the news reported that a jet had crashed into the North Tower of the World Trade Center in New York City.

As the live streaming of this catastrophic event continued, and just when we thought things couldn't get any worse, a second jet slammed into the South Tower! We just knew at that point that these were no accidents. The very freedom of the United States was now under attack. Just a little while later, the news broadcast switched over to Washington, DC, where a jet had slammed into the Pentagon. About thirteen minutes later, the South Tower of the World Trade Center collapsed! No too long after that, the other tower went crashing to the ground, leaving New York City in a cloud of dust, smoke, and perpetual darkness. It was a gruesome image to watch live and just thinking of how many deaths, injuries, and emotional and physical damage all of this caused was heart-stopping.

We then watched live as the news reporters passed along the information that United Flight 93 was hijacked. The plane went crashing to the ground in a field in western Pennsylvania and all forty-five people on board were killed.

Since we were working for a high-profile investment firm, the place was shut down and all employees were sent home. The nightmare of those events on that dark day the world will never forget. If you were old enough to remember this day, you can recall exactly where and who you were with as you watched these events unfold. You may perhaps even have lost a family member or a friend or know personally someone who has. I'll never forget watching those moments in my dad's office with him.

I thought what happened that day evoked the most emotion I was capable of. Years later, however, on the fourteenth anniversary of 9/11, I was with my dad once again, and my life did change forever. What happened years later stirred deep and painful emotions for me with a loss that only certain people can describe. This consists of losing someone that they love and know that life will never be the same again without that person. It is a sharp emotional pain within your heart and soul that can never truly heal, which I have never felt before, but I would feel it fourteen years later on this very day, and there really was no way to prepare for the sting.

All in all, I truly was what people considered me to be—a nice guy. I was the kind of guy who would walk into a bar, throw my credit card on the counter, and buy everyone a drink. First and foremost, though, I would always take care of my bartender, which of course has its own rewards. I would do just about anything for anyone, especially if they were in some kind of trouble.

I remember one time when I was living at my apartment and my sister was soon to be dropped off by her friend's mom. When they arrived, the mother was hysterical because she accidentally bumped into my car in the parking lot, scraped the paint, and messed up the bumper. I consoled her and said that it was fine and not to worry about it. This is the kind of guy that I am. I don't let silly things like that bother me, but with her persistence she ended up writing a check for a thousand dollars to cover the damages. I still said that it was okay, but she would not take no for an answer. I took the check, cashed it, got tattoos, and partied the rest of the money away. The car never got repaired, so you can see where my priorities were.

My personal rule of thumb pertaining to partying was if I could snort it, eat it, or smoke it, it was okay, but no needles. This was a code I lived by, which I held to tightly. I saw too many people die from overdoses using a needle, and I did not want to be a victim myself.

I had many girlfriends but no love for them like for my first true love. I had no idea that she and my dad had stayed in touch over the years until I saw a Christmas card she had sent to him. She really did not have a father figure in her life, and I do believe that she looked at him like a father. Out of the blue (with some persuasion by my dad, I am sure), I received a Christmas card from her, and we began talking again.

Things between the two of us went slowly; we formed a relationship, and we knew that we were still in love. It was a long-distance relationship, but we decided to make it serious. We decided to get engaged, and she was giving up her life, her job, and everything to be with me. Life seemed to be going in a good direction until I made the worst mistake and decided to go out for one last hoorah.

I got my second DUI. This time, as it so happens, I was three times over the legal limit.

Initially, I was ordered to be put on house arrest, report to a probation officer, and use a breathalyzer each time I started my car, which, by the way, I was only permitted to drive to and from work. I had decided to represent myself rather than retain a lawyer. As luck would have it, when I got to the courthouse, there was a problem with my paperwork, and I found myself on the way to jail: I was processed as an inmate (orange suit and all), and spent many long and arduous hours in a cell. Finally, I spoke with a social worker who cleared up the miscommunication. I was let go, and this was quite a wakeup call for me.

My fiancée stood by me in these tumultuous times; it was a long year. Subsequently, she took over handling my finances (because I was in deep credit card debt), and she found a job rather quickly.

I calmed down a lot in that time period, but when I got my license back, the bar scene was right back in my train of thought. I had lived most of my life in the drug and booze culture, and in all honesty, I had no idea how to have fun or socialize without being a part of it. Something good happens, go out and celebrate with a drink and get drugs! Something bad happens, sulk in pity with some drugs and booze. Bored? Go out to the bar just to kill time, and so on. How could someone who lived a life like this for so long drastically change everything by his or her own power? I mean this is all that I knew—how to have fun and how to pass the time.

My fiancée and I decided to discuss the options for a wedding and set a day. We bought a house together in the process, and shortly thereafter, I decided to go out on St. Patrick's Day, but not drive, and walk to the bar that was only two miles away. I was so new to the neighborhood that on the way home, I thought I knew where I was going, but being intoxicated probably did not help the situation. I figured I would take a shortcut home and hopped a fence to avoid a longer walk, but unbeknown to me, it was into someone's backyard! It was dark, it was cold, it was two thirty in the morning, and I landed in the backyard to a dog barking, a light blazing, and man pointing a gun with the barrel aimed directly at my face.

At gunpoint I was held hostage while his wife called the police. Apparently he thought I was going to rob him, but I drunkenly explained to him the situation, and he actually thought it was quite comical, especially since I was wearing a St. Patrick's Day shirt that read, "Kiss me, I'm hammered"; but it was too late—the police got there to pick me up, threw me in the drunk tank, and gave me a disorderly conduct charge, a public drunkenness charge, and a prowling charge.

In the newspapers, it reported that I was a prowler. I had many disorderly conducts on my record, two DUIs, and now a prowler charge on my permanent record.

I paid the fine and that was that, but being known to the public as a prowler was quite embarrassing: people wondered what I did. The worst was getting a call from my mom, who was an avid newspaper reader. I knew she would see the article and I would get a call at some point, and as it so happened that I was right.

As I explained to her what actually happened, I could tell that she was very hurt, and I am not really sure if she truly believed me. Nevertheless, I am sure that when her friends confronted her about seeing my name in the paper, it was not a very proud moment for her. When we do foolish things, we never think about the total outcome. When we hurt ourselves, we also hurt the ones we love.

In 2003, my father lost an aunt he was very close to, and a year later, he lost his favorite uncle, her husband. In their prime, the couple traveled the United States in their mobile home. They loved each other dearly, and they loved my dad like their own son. Needless to say, Dad took the news pretty hard. Unfortunately, they did not have any children; financially, they were well off, and Dad became their sole beneficiary. As a result, he bought a high-priced car he always wanted, and to everyone it was known as the Bat Mobile.

One thing you have to know about my dad is that he loved to take naps. This was a guy who could sleep just about anywhere at any given time. Sometimes it worked in his favor, and other times it did not. Around this time, my dad decided he wanted to go visit my older sister and her family in Georgia, but he was deathly afraid to fly. He did not want to drive the sixteen hours, so he decided to take a train. Long story short, he fell asleep, and when he woke up, he was in Miami, Florida! We all got a good laugh about that!

When he got back home, he noticed that there was something wrong with his stomach; in fact, it appeared as if there was something popping out of it. He went to his doctor and was told he had an aortic aneurysm and had to have surgery. Now, on top of his comical way of taking his false teeth out and leaving them in drinking cups at restaurants to get a rise out of people, he had a new joke. He called the bulge in his stomach the "green guy" in honor of the movie *Alien*. My dad had quite a sense of humor and made the best out of the worst situation.

About this time my boss at work was in the process of planning his wedding. He asked me to be his best man, and while I was honored, I told him I would only do it if he would be my best man at my wedding. We both agreed. We were really close, and I would not have traded his friendship in for anything in the world. He was always there for me, and he knew I was always there for him. It was a very happy day when he finally got married. I loved him, as well as his beautiful wife, very much.

My fiancée and I began to realize our American dream by planning our wedding. She was raised Roman Catholic, and I was raised with Christian ideas, so we began to go church shopping.

We found a Methodist church a couple of towns over from where we lived. We went to some services on Sundays, we liked the pastor, and we met with him to discuss a wedding ceremony. We went through a couple of hours of Christian counseling and continued to go to fellowship services on Sundays. We finally got married on June 3, 2006. It was one of the best days of my life.

Shortly thereafter, my dad had an abdominal hernia from the aneurism surgery, which brought along with it an atrial fibrillation, so his doctor began to closely monitor him with regular doctor appointments. It was nothing life-threatening, but it needed monitoring just the same.

As my dad's physical health slowly began to decline, I was very anxious for some good news. I got some when my wife and I found out that she was unexpectedly pregnant! We were very excited, things were going well, we had a house, my wife had a good job, and I was beginning to excel at my job. My boss began to be my mentor (he was an awesome boss, and I truly admired his leadership skills and style), and I worked hard, gradually moving up to management as a team leader, and then a supervisor, and was making exceptional money for someone who did not have a college degree. (I was actually making more money than my wife who had a college degree.) I really enjoyed what I was doing, and I calmed down a lot. The New York Giants ended up winning another Super Bowl in 2007, when I was thirty-one years old, and I was ready for just about anything, until something happened that forever changed my life.

CHAPTER 2

My Experiential Religious Experience or Testimony

Some people believe that this is the most powerful and persuasive form of an argument for defending the faith because it is a personal experience.

I just happen to agree, and you are about to learn about mine.

One night in 2008, I decided to go out and get drunk; I went to the same bar I walked to on St. Patrick's Day. Long story short, I woke up outside of the bar underneath a big rig truck in the cold and snow with a bloody lip, blood all over my coat, and no recollection from the night before. I lost my car keys, and according to my watch, I was going to be late for work.

I had many nights where I did not remember the night before, but this experience was different. It was a long, cold walk back home, and it was the first time in my life I had tears running from my eyes.

My cell phone was dead, and I could not call anyone. It weighed heavy on my mind—not just what had happened, but all the rotten things I had done in my life.

It was like a flash of conviction that ran through my thoughts and heart, and my entire life was being exposed to someone right before my very eyes on this walk.

I felt like I was standing alone, afraid, naked, and exposed for everyone to see. I had an overwhelming sense of guilt, and it was just consuming me. The only way I can possibly describe this feeling in words is that it was an extremely dirty feeling.

I did not understand what or why this was happening to me at the time, but when I look back on this true experience, I now know that it was the Holy Spirit convicting me of my sin. By doing this, God was actually showing His love for me. Now, this may sound foreign to someone who is not a Christian, but this is one of the functions of the Holy Spirit. From that moment on, I began a spiritual search and a quest for truth to find out what was going on.

I never had an issue believing that there was and is a god. Now that I look back at when I went through this part of my life, knowing that there is a Creator, I was like what Paul mentioned when he wrote his letter to the church in Romans 1:20, "For the invisible things of Him from the creation of the world are clearly seen, being understood by the things that are made, even His eternal power and Godhead; so that they are without excuse."

I had numerous spiritual conversations with various types of people who considered themselves spiritual in my life prior to this experience, especially when I was tripping on acid or shrooming on magic mushrooms, because they sure made me feel spiritual. As I said I was a very sociable person and open to any forms of conversation.

I welcomed and accepted all forms of religions and thought that they all were a path to God. So the problem for me was not an atheistic or agnostic approach to life, because I truly believed that there was a god. As my dad often said, "There has got to be somebody in charge up there." I even prayed to a god throughout my life very selfishly or when life just was not going my way.

The bottom line was that something happened to me that day, I wanted to know what it was, and the only explanation was some type of divine intervention that gave me this overpowering sense of shame within my conscience.

So this began my spiritual search. I had been to church many times throughout my life, so I first tried to look at things from a Christian perspective, which I really knew nothing about. The only thing in my life that could identify me with Christianity was when I was a Marine—they needed to know what denomination to put on my dog tags in case I was killed for a proper burial. I chose Methodist because that is what my dad told me to do and that is what he did.

He considered himself a Methodist because he went to a Methodist church when he was a kid.

In reality I did not understand the meaning of being a Christian and what the gospel truly meant. I was going through the motions like many others. I was a "Sunday Mist-ian," meaning I sat in church on Sundays and missed the point of being there (a word and meaning that I made up). I never understood the meaning of sin because no one took the time to tell me about it. I did not get the reasoning behind the mystery of Jesus Christ. I lived a life of ignorance, unbelief, and I gladly indulged in the sins of my generation. The sins were labeled as acceptable in my mind and just a part of growing up. I partook without hesitation, not because everyone else was doing it, but because it felt good.

So I then tried to pick up a Bible. The actual one I carried around when I was a kid. It was on the bookshelf, covered in dust, with funeral, prayer, and memorial cards in it, which was basically just a storage system for them. I began to read.

I tried and I tried, but I just could not understand any of it. I did not know where to begin, I was just so confused, and none of it made any sense. After many attempts, I gave up in serious frustration. All the while the overwhelming guilt of my past was consuming me.

I went on to do some serious and intense research on many religious systems and various subjects; you name it, I researched it. This is coming from a guy who hated to read but now wanted to. It was a very enlightening time in my life as I took in wall sorts of information that I had never been interested in before and learned a lot of my own free will.

I was seriously seeking to find out how the world viewed God, but wherever I looked, I could not find any type of relief within my conscience for the guilt I had been feeling and what happened to me that day.

I kept asking myself how all these faiths could not be rational about the problem I was having?

Was it possible that all of these faiths were wrong about their interpretation for their path to God?

I then began to deeply envision in my mind about death and what happens to the human body when it dies. It may sound morbid, but I just could not help the thoughts.

I had thoughts and questions such as: When you die is that just it, or does the body have a spirit or soul that moves on?

All of these religions that I was researching believed so, but all of these faiths just had no direct answers and were very sketchy.

It got me thinking about all the times that I had been in a cemetery and saw the countless number of tombstones.

The headstones were marked with people's first and last names, a date of birth and a date of death with a dash in between, with the dash telling the unknown, mysterious story of the individual's life.

One simple line summed up everything?

All the date of births and deaths varied—some people lived short lives, some longer lives; some were young, and some old.

It got me thinking about all the different ways that they possibly died, such as old age, disease, suicide, accident, and the list could go on, but they all had one thing in common: the end of their physical life.

They were all dead and buried six feet under the ground. They were all bodies of men and women, boys and girls, who lived and walked the earth at some point.

What was the point of life?

It just got me thinking that I would be dead one day too. There was no getting around this fact.

A lifeless, cold, physical body decaying inside of a box if that was my choice, or would I rather be cremated?

Would I get the chance to make that decision?

Death could creep up on me in an unexpected way—car crash, heart attack, or anything for that matter.

I started thinking about all the times that I could and should have died but escaped death and was able to pick up and live another day.

Why was I given that next day?

My friends, my family, my wife, sisters, mother, father, and even my unborn child would have their turns. There was no escaping death.

The thought of having a child made me think I was being selfish knowing that someday he or she would undergo possible pain, suffering, and then the inevitable death. As we watched our child take his or her first steps, as cute as it would be, it would be more steps closer to their last.

How could I bring a baby into the world knowing that someday he or she would have to face death?

It really bothered me.

There was no way around the fact that once you are born, you begin the dying process, and everyone would have a time where they would give up their last breath.

What was the point of life? Just to die?

Do all people think about these things?

Maybe not in the same context, but do they?

These questions kept weighing in on my mind as well as the guilt I still had, and all of it was consuming me. I fell into a bit of depression for the first time in my life. I spent much time alone and absorbed myself in reading about world religions and their views on death and the afterlife as well as atheism, and then things just got worse.

I started to think about the subject of heaven and hell.

Is there a heaven?

If there is, is there a hell?

If there was a hell, would I go there?

I thought I was a good person by secular standards. But did God think so?

I mean, I did a lot of good things, and the bad things I did happened in the past, so did they really matter now?

I had become a better person, cut down on drinking, did not do drugs anymore, had a good job, and was married, had a baby on the way, and faithful to my wife.

I began to research the subject of hell. Some religions believed in it and some didn't. Some believed in reincarnation and some did not even believe in a soul. I was brought back to where I started with this quest for truth and back to a Christian perspective on it.

I mean, what better person to go to than Jesus, who made the claim that He is the Way, the truth, and the Life, right?

Jesus saith unto him, I am the way, the truth, and the life: no man cometh unto the Father, but by Me. (John 14:6)

The person who claimed to have died, defeated death, and rose from the grave, right?

I am the resurrection, and the life: he that believeth in Me, though he were dead, yet shall he live. (John 11:25)

After intense research, the place called hell was now becoming a reality, and from what I was reading, I was heading there. The bottom line is that if there is a moral God (which I believed), then there is a moral law (which I did not understand), and God is the moral source for all of His creation (which I believed.)

This then began the argument from a moral position within my mind to try to justify my conscience. The problem was that I could not win this debate. I stood guilty as charged, and my conscience was convicting me and giving me this sense of overwhelming guilt that made me feel so dirty. Everywhere I turned I could not find relief.

I was beginning to realize that God is the only adequate explanation, source, and grounds for my absolute moral obligation because I repeatedly disobeyed my conscience. Easily defined, "con" means "with" and "science" means "knowledge," so "with knowledge" over and over again I disobeyed the true definition of conscience: the voice of God within my soul.

The *Young's Analytical Concordance to the Bible* brilliantly defines it as: "A knowing with oneself."

It then goes on to list every time *conscience* is mentioned throughout the Bible, which is thirty-four times, and the word is only mentioned in the New Testament. This may be because of the early Jews' awareness of the power of revealed truth through God's direct communication with them. This is only a theory and is a subject to debate within the Christian and Jewish community.

I then felt led to take a look at the Ten Commandments, the Decalogue, or the divine law in the Bible. They are listed twice, once in Exodus 20:1–17 and then in Deuteronomy 5:6–21.

In the New Testament, Paul refers to them as "written not with ink but with the Spirit of the living God; not in tables of stone, but in fleshly tables of the heart," in his second letter to the Corinthians.

Why have I singled out just the Ten Commandments here when the Old Testament lists over six hundred laws that include dietary guidelines, laws of nature, sacrificial animal regulations, and how to live as a community?

This is a fair question that deserves much-needed attention and actually has a very simple answer. The tablets of stone that have been mentioned do not say anymore, as we can see when Moses addressed the Ten Commandments:

> These words the LORD spake unto all your assembly in the mount out of the midst of the fire, of the cloud, and of the thick darkness, with a great voice: and He added no more. And He wrote them in

two tables of stone, and delivered them unto me.
(Deuteronomy 5:22)

To my understanding, the phrase "He added no more" is
of the upmost importance to the issue of moral obligation.

So what are the Ten Commandments?

All I knew was thou shalt not lie, steal, and honor your
parents. I knew there were seven more and that most of
them began with the same three famous and unforgettable
words imbedded in many human beings minds all over the
world: "Thou shalt not°…"

The Ten Commandments are as follows:

1. "Thou shalt have none other gods before Me."

When I first read this commandment, I did not really
understand it. Then I really thought about it and knew
that "other gods" referred to my selfish interests. I never put
God first in my life. I actually only prayed when I needed
something, which is selfish ambition.

2. "Thou shalt not make thee any graven image, or any
likeness of anything that is in heaven above, or that is
in the earth beneath, or that is in the waters beneath the
earth."

When I first looked at the words "graven image," they did
not make sense to me, but a synonym is the word *idolatry*,
and it can be defined as creating your own image of God in

your mind that you are more comfortable with. I did this all of my life, redefining God as an image that suited me and not understanding that I was created out of His image and not the other way around. The God I created overlooked my sins.

3. "Thou shalt not take the name of the Lord thy God in vain."

I think that there was a time in my life that every other word that came out of my mouth profaned the name of God. Sometimes it was intentional and other times it was not; either way, I was guilty.

4. "Keep the Sabbath day to sanctify it."

I never in my entire life took one day out of seven to reflect on God and pay tribute and praise Him. I had been to church, but it was forced on me, or I was there with an ulterior motive. Such was the case when my wife and I were trying to get in good with the church we liked and wanted the pastor of the church to conduct our ceremony. We only did it because we thought that the church was beautiful both inside and out, especially for pictures.

5. "Honor thy father and thy mother."

Looking back on my life, I truly had to admit that I had not always honored my parents. I loved them dearly, but I dishonored them in many ways—some they both knew about and some they did not. I could just imagine the pain they felt every time they read my name in the newspaper for a DUI, disorderly conduct, or the one time with the prowling charge, how much embarrassment it must have caused each of them! It pains me just to think about it.

6. "Thou shalt not kill."

Now here was one that I thought I got off pretty easy. I have never hunted or killed a deer; maybe I stepped on an ant or two, but I'd never murdered anything or anyone. But on further reflection, I remembered my many sexual encounters with women before I got married. I had been with married women and women who had boyfriends. In a particular instance, a pregnancy test came up positive. Since there were possible multiple partners involved, I cannot say for sure that I was the father, although the possibility was there, and I had consented to help with an abortion process.

The woman ended up getting the abortion, we lost touch, and that whole experience is something I have to live with for the rest of my life. Not knowing if the baby was mine weighs heavily on my conscience even to this day. Even at the time I knew in my heart that I would have to answer to God about that someday. It pains me to think about it and know that I could have been part of consenting to the death of my child. It just brings me to tears to think about it.

I then also looked into the fact on how murdering someone in Gods eyes can have two meanings. The physical act of taking one's life, or a simple thought of hate. Jesus said in 1 John 3:15, "Whosoever hateth his brother is a murderer: and ye know that no murderer hath eternal life abiding in him."

This is where I felt there were many gray areas. I have told many people that I hated them, felt it in my heart when I was betrayed, and truly hated many people.

7. "Neither shalt thou commit adultery."

Though I have never cheated on my wife, before I was married I had to be honest with myself and understand that I had slept with many married women. Though it was in the past, that did not get me off scot-free. I was now only beginning to understand that marriage is a solemn vow to God to remain faithful to your lifelong partner. Breaking the covenant is a sin. But adultery can also have another view that Jesus expounds on in Matthew 5:28 and can be as simple as a look or a thought: "But I say unto you, That whosoever looketh on a woman to lust after her hath committed adultery with her already in his heart."

I began to think about all the women I had looked at lustfully, always undressing them with my eyes, and all the strip clubs I had been to and all the pornographic films that I had seen in my life just seemed too high to even number. My pornography video and magazine collection all were visual proof that there certainly was a problem in that area.

8. "Neither shalt thou steal"

I had to really think about this. I never robbed a bank, but there I was trying to justify my actions and comparing myself to others who may have stolen higher-value items. I, as well as many other unbelievers, tend to do this when comparing any sin I commit to other people's sins. Maybe this is in contrast to what Jesus said in Matthew 7:1–5:

> Judge not, that ye be not judged. For with what judgment ye judge, ye shall be judged: and with what measure ye mete, it shall be measured to you again. And why beholdest thou the mote that is in thy brother's eye, but considerest not the beam that is in thine own eye? Or how wilt thou say to thy brother, Let me pull out the mote out of thine eye; and, behold, a beam is in thine own eye? Thou hypocrite, first cast out the beam out of thine own eye; and then shalt thou see clearly to cast out the mote out of thy brother's eye.

And in Luke 6:41–42:

> And why beholdest thou the mote that is in thy brother's eye, but perceivest not the beam that is in thine own eye? Either how canst thou say to thy brother, Brother, let me pull out the mote that is in thine eye, when thou thyself beholdest not the beam that is in thine own eye? Thou hypocrite, cast out first the beam out of thine own eye, and then shalt thou see clearly to pull out the mote that is in thy brother's eye.

I remember many times stealing things that seemed to be of no value, but the fact of the matter is that the item did not belong to me and I willfully took it. I took someone else's idea and got credit for it, took things home from work, took money off of a bar, and I realized that I didn't need to rob a bank to be a thief!

9. "Neither shalt thou bear false witness against thy neighbor."

Being honest with myself, I had to admit that I had told many lies and was the king of exaggerating stories. Though there may have been some truth in them, an exaggeration is a sugar-coated lie. I thought about all the white lies I had told, and it did not really matter what I called them because they were still lies. A lie is a lie—it does not matter how many or how little they are. I was a liar!

10. "Neither shalt thou desire (covet) thy neighbour's°…"

–I had heard the word *covet* once or twice before in my life, but I never knew what it meant. After looking into it, it basically means desiring something that does not belong to you. Being honest with myself once again, I had to come to the conclusion that I was guilty. My entire life was based on going for things that did not belong to me. All the married women that I slept with! They belonged to their husbands and vice versa. They had made a solemn vow to each other, and I jumped in the middle of that. It brought me to tears to think about how many times I did this, as well as coveting material things. I stood guilty as charged.

So there I was. I took an honest approach within my heart and looked at all of the Ten Commandments. I broke not just one or two of them; I had broken them all!

And then it got worse as I saw Paul go on to list other types of people that would not inherit the kingdom of God. What really stood out to me was *drunkard* and *fornicator.*

> Know ye not that the unrighteous shall not inherit the kingdom of God? Be not deceived: neither fornicators, nor idolaters, nor adulterers, nor effeminate, nor abusers of themselves with mankind, Nor thieves, nor covetous, nor drunkards, nor revilers, nor extortioners, shall inherit the kingdom of God. (1 Corinthians 6: 9-10)

I was a drunkard! I did not understand what a *fornicator* was, so I looked it up. According to the *Merriam-Webster Dictionary,* fornication means "consensual sexual intercourse between two persons not married to each other."

To think that there were men and women in the world that could count the amount of people that they had sex with on one hand was foreign to me. Some people count sheep to make themselves fall asleep at night, and I would try to count and name the amount of women that I slept with to make myself tired. I would lose track after about sixty! Fornication was a sin and reality that I never thought about, which put me in a state of depression like I had never been in before. But as I continued to read 1 Corinthians 6, it went on to say in verse 11, "And such were some of you: but ye are washed, but ye are sanctified, but ye are justified in the name of the Lord Jesus, and by the Spirit of our God."

All of this information was beginning to make sense. Just when I thought that I had nowhere to turn, I realized that the Ten Commandments demonstrated that "we have all sinned" (Romans 3:23) and are therefore in need of God's mercy and grace, which is only available through faith in Jesus Christ.

I had heard it all before but never listened. It was now finally making sense.

It did not matter whether I did sins in secret; I would be judged for them.

For God shall bring every work into judgment, with every secret thing, whether it be good, or whether it be evil. (Ecclesiastes 12:14)

One of my biggest problems was that I thought only bad people went to a place called hell. I thought because I was basically a good person, I would go to a place called heaven when I died. You know, the place that we have all been told about where we sit on puffy, white clouds with angels that looked like babies with wings playing harps, jumping from cloud to cloud for eternity?

You know this place, right?

The place that we have all been told about that *does not exist.*

You see, the word *good* to the secular world is very different, because the Bible says in Romans 3:12, "They are all gone out of the way, they are together become unprofitable; there is none that doeth good, no, not one."

Despite what people thought of me or what I thought of myself, according to what I was reading and feeling, I was not very good at all.

There was no amount of good works or righteous acts that I could do to cover up the bad in my life. "But we are all as an unclean thing, and all our righteousnesses are as filthy rags; and we all do fade as a leaf; and our iniquities, like the wind, have taken us away" (Isaiah 64:6).

The way in this verse portrays filthy rags refers to the cloths women used during menstruation a time long ago, when they were considered unclean in the ceremonial sense.

My sin would not be overlooked, it could not go unpunished, and I could now finally see that I deserved punishment. God was not going to send me to hell; I was willfully sending myself there because God is just and holy, and I was the complete opposite. I finally took a look at God's view of good according to the Christian faith and realized that I was not good at all.

And it's not just me—we will all be judged, both believers and unbelievers.

Revelation 20:11–15 speaks about "the great white throne."

2 Corinthians 5:10 speaks about "the judgment seat of Christ."

Paul in the following verse calls this judgment seat the "Terror of the Lord": "Knowing therefore the terror of the

Lord, we persuade men; but we are made manifest unto God; and I trust also are made manifest in your consciences" (2 Corinthians 5:11).

Wow! I really was beginning to understand a lot of things about my conscience!

Sin is not just about breaking a book of rules—it goes a lot deeper. It is about knowing where or how we can do as good and not doing it: "Therefore to him that knoweth to do good, and doeth it not, to him it is sin" (James 4:17).

I then took a good look at the book of Romans 7–12. This really hit a nerve in my conscience.

These are the real issues with conscience and morality. The moral law is written on our hearts, and there is no escaping this:

> For when the Gentiles, which have not the law, do by nature the things contained in the law, these, having not the law, are a law unto themselves: Which shew the work of the law written in their hearts, their conscience also bearing witness, and their thoughts the mean while accusing or else excusing one another;) In the day when God shall judge the secrets of men by Jesus Christ according to my gospel. (Romans 2:14–16)

I wanted to be forgiven. I now knew that the only way to get forgiveness and be cleansed was through the blood of Christ.

Days progressed and I was still overwhelmed with guilt, but things were beginning to make sense for me. I knew what I had to do, but it would take a great step of faith, which I knew that I really did not have.

I decided to try to talk to someone about all of this, and the only person I could think of was the pastor from the church that married my wife and me. I called him, made an appointment, and then I went to see him.

I told him about what was going on, and I could not believe his reaction. He told me that hell was basically just a metaphor, and a place called hell really did not exist. Everyone in all faiths will end up going to heaven. What we read in the Bible is true, but a lot of the things we read are just metaphors. The conversation was not productive at all, and I left there in a state of confusion like I had never experienced.

I mean, he was a nice guy and all, but he was a pastor, claimed to be a leader of the Christian faith, and he did not believe in hell? Here was a man with a seminary degree, well-respected in the community, and his Christian church embraced the concept of universalism? As I look back on this experience, I am just pretty much hurt over it. I mean, I was drowning, and all he had to do was throw me a lifeline, which was Jesus, but the offer never came.

In my mind, when I died I would be left in the hands of the living God, which as Hebrews 10:31 describes as a fearful thing:

"It is a fearful thing to fall into the hands of the living God."

He could and should have given me the only mediator there is:

> Who will have all men to be saved, and to come unto the knowledge of the truth. For there is one God, and one mediator between God and men, the man Christ Jesus; Who gave Himself a ransom for all, to be testified in due time. (1 Timothy 2:4–6)

About a week later, I decided to find out if all of this Jesus stuff was for real.

On December 8, 2008, I got down on my knees in my living room. It was early in the afternoon, no one was home, and I really did not know what I was doing.

With tears in my eyes, I repented with godly sorrow for all that I had done in my life, asked Jesus to cleanse me of my sin, and asked Him to come into my life and be my Lord and Savior. I then forgave myself and said from there on out I wanted to be a new person.

This was an act of faith and a very humbling experience, especially doing it alone and coming to the conclusion that I had sinned against God and was at His mercy.

At the time when I did it, I did not think it was going to do anything, even though I meant every word.

I did not see fireworks or see a sign.

When I opened my eyes and dried the tears from my face, I did not feel any different.

I didn't even tell anyone what I had done; they all would have thought I had completely lost it, which I was beginning to think might be true.

The following day, without an alarm clock going off, I woke up at exactly 4:00 a.m. Now this was quite early for me because I liked to sleep in as long as I could. I was wide awake and walked out to my living room and stood right in the spot where I had asked Jesus into my life.

I looked around at the dark, quiet, chilly room and couldn't figure out why I was up; most of all, I was wondering why I wasn't even tired.

I sat down on my couch, trying to figure out why I was up, and then looked on the table and saw the Bible sitting there; the one that I had tried and tried to read but just could not understand.

I don't know how to explain it, but at that very moment I felt a tug in my heart to pick it up and give it another shot.

I opened it, flipped through the pages a little bit, and then stopped in the New Testament at the gospel of Luke.

I then began to read and could not believe my eyes because I understood everything that I read!

It was like an internal light had gone on!

I was at a loss for words°…

What I had needed was Jesus in my life before I could understand God's word, and the Bible confirms this truth in 1 Corinthians 2:14: "But the natural man receiveth not the things of the Spirit of God: for they are foolishness unto him: neither can he know them, because they are spiritually discerned."

I was now no longer a natural man, but a person with the spirit of God. And the Holy Spirit began to speak to me through God's word.

Sound crazy?

If it does, I completely understand. At first I thought I was going insane and kept this enlightening experience to myself. I did not want anyone to think that I had gone mad and turned into a Bible thumper, especially with a baby on the way.

The truth is that as I read the Bible, it confirmed that I was forgiven, cleansed, new, and ready for a new life, and I could not put it down!

What takes a typical human being with dedication about a year to do— reading the Bible from the beginning to the end—I did in two and half months. I then began to study it more in-depth, and I saw many changes within myself happen. Ever since that fateful day when I woke up at four in the morning, I have continued to read the Bible daily.

Through reading the Bible I understood that it is not based on feelings but on promises. My guilt went away, and I was able to focus on the promises. It was like a heavy weight had been lifted off of my shoulders.

The word of God changed my life and began to give me answers to a lot of life's most difficult questions.

When I first began my quest for truth, I looked into so many different world religions for the right path to God, but what I learned is that there is no right path to God, and this is why other religions cannot work. It is man's hopeless search, and you need Christ.

> For this is good and acceptable in the sight of God our Saviour; Who will have all men to be saved, and to come unto the knowledge of the truth. For there is one God, and one mediator between God and men, the man Christ Jesus; Who gave himself a ransom for all, to be testified in due time. (1 Timothy 2:3–6)

So here I was with my life changed; what do I do now?

What does anyone want to do when they receive good news and a major life change for the better?

They want to share it with everyone so that they too can participate in their joy, or so I thought.

CHAPTER 3

Beginning My Life as a Believer

So there I was, thirty-two years old, a proud father of a precious baby girl, and I was now a Christian. Talk about some major life changes for me. I had such a new zeal for life in general. I was getting up early, studying the Bible, being a dad, being a husband, enjoying my job, and it was all because of Jesus.

I suppose one would think that the next step for someone in my position would be to begin to look for a church. Well, I did not. I was more like an independent Christian and wanted to explore some things before I even thought about finding a church.

What I wanted to learn more about was other religions and the history of Christianity, and by this I mean the early church. I really don't know why I felt pulled in this direction, but I felt that I needed to for some reason. Though I intensely studied some when the Holy Spirit convicted me, I really wanted to go in-depth. I started to go to the bookstore and buy many books on all kinds of subjects to compare them from a Christian perspective. I immersed myself in subjects such as the Jehovah's Witness, the Mormons (better known as the Church of Jesus Christ of Latter-day Saints), Christian Science, the Theosophical Society, Buddhism, The Baha'i Faith, the new age cults, the Unification Church, Scientology, agnosticism, atheism, Hinduism, Rajneeshism, ISKCON-International Society for Krishna Consciousness/ Hare Krishna's, TM (Transcendental Meditation), the apocalyptic cults, Islam, Unitarian Universalism, and evolution.

My brain became like a sponge, and I just soaked everything in. I wanted to know everything about what anyone could possibly believe and why they were not Christians!

At this point in my life, I had to tell someone what was going on, and the best person to talk to was my wife. After a long conversation, I really don't think she believed what I was saying and wanted to see if it was true by watching what kind of impact it had on my life.

She noticed a change in me. I did not go out to the bar anymore, I stopped hanging out with friends who may have a bad influence on me, I was reading the Bible daily, along with other religion books that were scattered everywhere, I was talking about spiritual things, watching Christian-based messages on television, and changed my whole taste in music to Christian contemporary rock. I would get upset when she used my car and left the radio on a country music channel.

Here was a guy who used to listen to music like the Slayer album *God Hates Us All* going to the other extreme of loving "I Can Only Imagine" by MercyMe. I stopped using profanity and threw all of my pornographic films in the garbage. She truly saw a change in me and knows for a fact that my experience was real and in no way, shape, or form was I making it up. In all honesty, why would I?

I then shared my experience with my mother, father, and two sisters. My mother was a Christian, so she was very happy for me. My two sisters and my father, on the other hand, thought it was just a stage I was going through and I would be back to my normal crazy self as soon as it was over. My dad told his cousin who is a Christian about my experience, and she sent me a gift in the mail of a NIV Life Application Study Bible. It was so helpful to me at that stage in my life.

After about a little under a year of being solo, I decided it was time to look for a church, and boy, I had no idea what I was getting myself into. I had no clue about the differences in denominations or the Roman Catholic Church. All I knew was the Bible, and you would figure that would be enough, but the Christian confusion set in!

I decided to go to churches in the area and sit in on some services. Clearly the church where I gotten married and had the conversation with the pastor was completely out of the question. Some other churches and services I enjoyed and some just seemed not biblical at all.

I settled in at a Baptist church for a few services, spoke with the pastor through e-mail, but still did not feel at home.

My mother knew that I was church shopping, and a friend of hers who was a Christian told her to tell me to look for a Wesleyan church because that seemed like the denomination I was looking for.

I took her advice, and by the grace of God, there was one less than two miles from my house. I began to go to services, Bible studies, got to know the pastor very well, and we became immediate friends.

I told him that I wanted to be baptized. He said that he would love to have the honor, and he was actually going to have a baptism service soon. I went to a few classes and learned about the importance of a believer's baptism according to the Wesleyan tradition.

The pastor told me that I would have to say something into a microphone in front of the congregation before he baptized me. I told him that I was scared to death to speak in public and probably could not say much, but he said that it was fine and just to say whatever came to mind.

I told my family I was going to get baptized and wanted them there to see it. My sisters and my mom were happy to come, but my dad could not understand why I wanted to get baptized since I had already been baptized as a baby. He said that I needed to think more about getting my daughter baptized instead.

That really confused me because I had read the Bible and did not see anything in it about infant baptism. The only mention of baptism was when someone would repent, which means to review one's actions and feel contrition or regret for past wrongs. When someone became a believer, in the Bible the words *repent* and *believe* are used, and a baby is incapable of doing this.

In the case of Lydia when she was converted by Paul's preaching, Acts 16:15 said, "And when she was baptized, and her *household*…"(italics mine).

And the Philippian jailer whom Paul and Silas had converted to the faith: "And he took them the same hour of the night, and washed their stripes; and was baptized, he and all his, *straightway*" (Acts 16:33, italics mine). The New King James Version substitutes the word *straightway* for *family*.

And in his greetings to the Corinthians, Paul said, "And I baptized also the *household* of Stephanas: besides, I know not whether I baptized any other" (1 Corinthians 1:16, italics mine).

In these three scripture references the word *household*, *family*, or *straightway* are used. Obviously, this means more than just the spouse was baptized, but to assume that babies were baptized as well is tough for me to grasp. I could see the possibility of children who were of an age where they could repent and believe being baptized, but a baby? The references could have also been about a slave who was part of the family.

This is where many Christians differ with theology (the study of Christian belief and practice) and tradition (the collection of practices and beliefs that develop over time), which I was ignorant of and had to do some investigating on these topics.

So finally on October 11, 2009, the day of my baptism came, and fear just set in my heart as I walked into the church to see the congregation and my family sitting there. I was happy to get baptized but mortified that I had to speak in public.

Anyhow, the time came when the pastor called me up front, and we walked to the baptismal tank. The worship leader sang a song and announced my name to everyone. He then said, "Bill, would you like to say something?"

I nearly passed out from fright. I looked out over the congregation, caught a glimpse of my dad sleeping and my mom nudging him to wake up and my two sisters looking on intently. I grabbed the microphone and said:

Good morning. When our pastor initially asked about if anyone was interested in being baptized, I jumped at the opportunity! He asked me if I was ready for this public proclamation of faith. I told him that I was so ready to the point that I would like to move the baptismal tank to Lincoln Financial field while wearing a New York Giants jersey and have him baptize me at half-time during an Eagles game for the world to see! And being a New York Giants fan it would be a pretty rough crowd.

Being baptized is one of the most important acts for me to address as a new Christian and believer. The most important act that I have completed was accepting Jesus Christ as my

Lord and Savior and repenting with godly sorrow for all of my sin on December eighth of last year. As the Bible states in 2 Corinthians 5:17, "Therefore, if anyone is in Christ, he is a new creation; the old has gone, the new has come!"

From that moment on, I truly believe that I was forgiven and became a new creation in Christ. It was like a huge weight was lifted off of my shoulders! God gave me a new heart and new desires. At one time in my life I was governed by sin, selfishness, Satan, and my senses. Upon conversion, God put His law in my mind, gave me the mind of Christ, and renewed me in the spirit of my mind. I am led by the Spirit, walking in His ways.

It is truly the most wonderful gift that could ever happen to me. I am born again!

All I want to do is evangelize to everyone who does not know the Lord. I was living in the dark for so long, and finally the light went on and I praise God for this. I now have been given the ability to read, study, and most importantly understand God's word. It is a new world for me, and it is so beautiful! Before I repented, God did not allow me to understand His word, and this I have come to realize was because the sin in my life was not yet forgiven. I now trust Him in everything and know that He is in control of my life.

I start my day daily with the word of God. I have committed myself solely to glorify His name. It is so true what the Bible says in Proverbs 8:17: "I love those who love me, and those who seek me find me," and Jeremiah 29:13: "You will seek me and find me when you seek me with all your heart."

I have finally found what was missing in my life—Jesus Christ.

I now need to surround myself with believers. A lot of people that I associate with, like coworkers, friends, and some family, do not know the Lord, and I pray for them daily. I do my best to open the gospel to them, but their hearts are hardened because God has not yet opened their hearts to Him, but I pray that He will in His own time. They think that I am most likely going through a phase and it will pass. But being born again is not a phase. It is a new birth! What I must do is set an example as a true Christian and plant the seed of the gospel. It is up to the Holy Spirit to then unharden the heart.

By no means do I think that being a Christian is better than anyone, it is completely the opposite. I have realized that there is nothing I can do to save myself from the wrath of God, except put my full trust in Christ. This is the difference in Christianity and "works based" religions. We realize that we are sinners, and everyone will be judged when we give God an account of our lives.

In Romans 14:11–12, it is written, "'As surely as I live,' says the Lord, 'every knee will bow before me; every tongue will confess to God.' So then, each of us will give an account of himself to God."

This is not a team effort. We all will individually give an account to God of our lives. We cannot earn our salvation with good deeds.

In <u>Isaiah 64:6</u>, it says all of us have become like one who is unclean, and all our righteous acts are like *filthy rags*; we all shrivel up like a leaf, and like the wind our sins sweep us away.

I put my full trust in Christ.

I have been looking for a church to worship at for some time now. I believe in my heart that I found the one I have been looking for. Our pastor is truly an amazing pastor, and all of you are so welcoming, and I thank you for that! I look toward the future to worship among you and grow with the Lord and the church.

God bless you all. Thank you and especially my family: my beautiful wife, my gorgeous baby girl Chesney Jane, and my mother, father, and sisters for being able to share this special moment in my life!

At this point the worship leader said in his microphone, "Well, I'll be. I think we have ourselves an up-and-coming pastor in the works."

It was strange, but I felt very at home in front of everyone. I felt comfortable, and the fear of speaking in front of people was gone. I never thought that could happen.

I was baptized in the name of the Father, and of the Son, and of the Holy Spirit, and it brought tears of joy to my eyes.

After the service, what my dad said to me really bothered me about getting my daughter baptized. The next thing that I knew my wife's family was calling her and asking when our daughter was going to get baptized.

This was something I really did not give much thought to, so I decided to talk it over with my pastor.

We had a great conversation; it was very fruitful, and I learned a lot. Because I had not done any research about Catholicism, I was ignorant of their beliefs about infant baptism.

I did not agree with it, and I did think that the baptism should only be for a believer. My pastor said there were only two solutions; either I made a stand in my faith, which could cause major family issues, or I could use a biblical principle to solve the issue. In Ephesians 4:3, it says, "Make every effort to keep the unity of the Spirit through the bond of peace."

I thought about it for a moment, realized I was strong in the faith but just not yet well-educated, did not have enough knowledge about differences in theology and tradition, was not ready to have a possible family feud over issues that I was not capable of backing up regarding Christian theology, and then thought putting Ephesians 4:3 into practice was the best idea at the time.

According to Catholicism, when a baby gets baptized, godparents are given to guide them in life. I respected that, so my wife and I made the decision to ask my older sister and her husband to be the godparents. They were Catholic too, and they were more than happy to take on the role.

I let my pastor baptize my daughter, all the family was there, and my older sister and her husband flew out from Georgia (because that is where they moved from Queens, New York) to be there. It was a beautiful ceremony, everyone was happy, and there was peace within the family.

A couple of days later, I had just gotten home from work when my very friendly neighbor who I knew was a Christian called me over to his porch.

We struck up a friendly conversation, and after a few minutes, he had asked if I heard about another neighbor on our street who was dying.

I told him that I had not. I asked him if the dying man was a Christian. I asked him if he had Jesus Christ as his Lord and Savior so he could die in peace and be sure of his eternal destination in heaven. I asked him if he knew how much God loved him. I asked him about his eternal salvation. I asked him many things until he stopped me in my tracks and said the most horrifying thing I could ever hear that could come out of a professing Christian's mouth. He said, "You need not concern yourself with matters like that. That is none of your business. It is up to the church and their responsibility."

He was an older Christian, in his late seventies, and I was not ready to argue. I was not equipped enough at the time to rip his un-Christianlike statement apart, because we were and are the church—*we are* the Body of Christ!

God spoke to me through him, and he was clearly wrong. It got me thinking about how many other professing Christians were out there who thought like this?

It weighed very heavily on my heart, mind, soul, and conscience from that day forward and gave me a burning desire from within.

Things in my life were going pretty great now. I became a member of the Wesleyan church and was even elected as an elder by the congregation, which I happily accepted.

At work things were going good, and then we found out that our company lost the contract and a new company was coming in. This had happened before, actually two other times, and it had worked out to my benefit. My boss and I were offered positions and even got a raise the other times.

This time was a little different. We both got offered a position, but we had to take a pay cut. We were both devastated, and there was nothing we could do.

It was going to be harder to pay bills for my family, and if I had accepted one of those false prosperity-health-and-wealth gospel messages that I saw on television that misguided so many people, I probably would have given up the faith too; however, I did not.

CHAPTER 4

Maturing in the Faith

As I matured as a Christian, I really felt distant from my father. We just did not have anything in common anymore. I loved him with all of my heart, we had been through a lot together, I could confide in him about anything, but the problem was our interests were no longer the same, and our entire perspectives on life were clearly different.

One of the negative realities about my dad was that he really enjoyed gambling. The big problem with it was that he had a very addictive personality and really did not know when to stop. He liked to host poker parties at his house, and though I would go once in a while, it was not to participate but to just spend time with him and see him have fun. He was a very charismatic guy, and when he was around his friends and in his element, he was a lot of fun to be around. I really was not opposed to gambling, if you can keep it in good fun, but he had a serious issue with it. The issue was extreme, especially since he also liked to go to Atlantic City sometimes for the weekend.

He liked to consider himself like a high roller and played the slot machines. I went with him once to Atlantic City when I was not a Christian, and even then it really was depressing for me. Not just watching him, but everyone else just looking for that lucky pull. You could see it in people's eyes on who truly had the gambling problem. Not that I was trying to judge, but it was very obvious.

After I became a Christian, he would still ask me to come along, but I could not bring myself to do it. I did not like to gamble. I truly thank God for that. If I played the penny slots and lost five dollars, I would feel so bad about it. Here was my dad playing twenty-dollar slots and hitting the ATM machine whenever he ran out of money, all the while having that look in his eye. I often heard horror stories when he got back from a trip from whoever he went with about how it was almost impossible to get him out of the casino.

We did have dinner together now and then, I would go to his place to visit with him often, he would also stop by to visit me, my wife, and my daughter, and I would also see him at work every day. We also would not allow anything to come between our tradition of getting together for football season and the New York Giants games, and it was not like we were growing apart, but my faith was so important to me, and he could not understand it.

He was sometimes very hostile toward Christianity and would not take the time to listen to me defend my position. He would make very negative assertions but then would not take the time to listen to what I had to say in response.

It was a one-sided argument most of the time and not very fair to say the least.

I knew that I would have to confront opposition at times, but from my dad it was very bothersome. He was so opinionated and not open to discussion. It was his way or no way at all.

As much as I tried to share the gospel with him, he clearly was not listening to what I was saying. Sometimes he tried to make conversation, but he truly was not interested in the details. He was sharp and quick with clever, negative, pop culture anti-Christian discourses, even if they did not really make sense or pertain to the situation at hand. His favorite argument was that he has been to church and considered himself a Christian, and he was in fact a Methodist. My instant response was a quote by a famous evangelist Billy Sunday (1862–1935), who gave up a professional baseball career to preach the gospel: "Going to church doesn't make you a Christian any more than going to a garage makes you an automobile."

Since my dad was sharp, tricky, and the king of one-liners, I figured it was time to start giving him a taste of his own medicine by being a bit clever with a little sarcasm myself.

Just when I thought I was making a breakthrough, he would change the subject or even begin to mock. This is common when people are ignorant of a subject. They feel cornered, and they will do just about anything not to address the topic that is being discussed. My dad was an exceptional case because he was someone who claimed to be a Christian but clearly was not by the way he lived and what he thought about issues of morality. He clearly was not honestly searching for answers, because if he was, he would take the time to listen.

Typical conversations with him would not be very lengthy. I'll share one below that we had that was actually a good one, if you can have a good spiritual conversation with him.

Dad: "Son, how do you know there really is a God?"

(Notice how I did not bring up the conversation?)

Me: "Well, Dad, I told you about my experience, and it was the moral law that convicted me of my sin. If there is a moral law, then there is a moral law giver, and that moral law giver could only be God. There are also many other factors that point to a Creator. I mean look at creation itself. It seems to me that°..."

(I then would be cut off.)

Dad: "Yeah, yeah, laws, shmaws, but all laws are different everywhere. What breaks the law here in the United States might not break the law in another country. So all laws are different. Who is to say that one law is right and one law is wrong? Seems to be like different cultures vary in laws. I was in the Drug Enforcement Agency and have been all over the world and have seen it firsthand on how laws are different."

Me: "That is a great point, and I am glad you brought it up. Look at what Hitler and his followers did. Do you think they were right killing millions of Jews?"

Dad: "No, but°..."

Me: "No buts about it. Do you personally feel and think that murdering millions of innocent Jewish people, including women and children, is wrong?"

Dad: "Yes, because murder is wrong."

Me: "Well, obviously Hitler and his followers did not agree with you, but they are in a different country, so does that mean they are right?"

Dad: "That is different. Do you want to go get lunch?"

Me: "Why is it different? You know at the Nuremberg trials Nazi officers' defense was that they were only acting under orders. I mean we were in the Marine Corps, so what if we were under orders to kill millions of innocent women and children? Would that make it right?"

Dad: "Are we going to go get lunch? I think we are done talking about this."

Me: "Seriously? Why can't we just finish this conversation? I mean, you brought it up. Listen, obviously sometimes 'I was only following orders' is not going to work. You have to be held accountable for your actions. Even at the Nuremberg trials this idea was rejected. It was said that 'people must obey a higher law if the law of the land is completely immoral. Murder can never be justified, even when the government approves of its practice.' Where does this higher law come from, Dad?"

Dad: "Well, that does not answer my question of why there are so many denominations. I think it is probably because Christians are wrong. Anyhow, let's go get some lunch; I'm hungry."

Me: "You just entirely changed the subject! What do denominations have to do with what we were talking about?"

Dad: "I'm just saying since there are so many of them, Christians can't get along, so Christianity must not be true. Do you want me to drive or do you want to?"

Me: "I'll drive, but I look at denominationalism completely different than you. I think that denominations are just based on disagreements over the interpretation of scripture and should just be an internal problem within the Body of Christ. I mean what family doesn't have problems? Look at our family—we have our own issues, but we resolve our differences within our family. Our neighbors, coworkers, friends, and people we don't interact with don't know the details of our problems. I do believe that the Body of Christ should be able to work out our differences within the Church, but unfortunately that does not happen. Think about how the media uses our differences against Christians to show that we are not unified in our purpose. Do you see what I am getting at?"

Dad: "No, but I really don't care. I'm starving."

Me: "Well, let's go then. But just think about this. Just because we can see celebrity family shows on television, and I know you watch them, exposing all of their internal problems for the viewer's entertainment, this does not mean they don't love each other. Plus I know you don't want me quoting the Bible, but this is very important. Jesus does preach unity within the Body of Christ, but we are humans and fail miserably. At least within a denominational setting everyone in attendance and having fellowship together are like-minded, are in one accord, and the Bible does say to do this. (For reference purposes I was referring to Philippians 2:1–2: "If there be therefore any consolation in Christ, if any comfort of love, if any fellowship of the Spirit, if any bowels and mercies, Fulfil ye my joy, that ye be likeminded, having the same love, being of one accord, of one mind." But I did not include this conversation.) Dad, does that make sense?"

Dad: "Well, you're a Wesleyan, and I'm a Methodist, so this means we shouldn't like each other. I remember growing up, on Sundays, the Protestants would walk on one side of the street and the Catholics on the other. We didn't like each other."

Me: "Geez, Dad, that is wrong in so many ways. I do believe that true Christians have a lot more in common than you think. For instance, it is not a matter of Catholics not liking Protestants, or the fact of me being a Wesleyan and you going to a Methodist church growing up—they are both Protestant. Look at John Wesley! He was actually known as one of the founders of Methodism and the Methodist movement. So even though Wesleyanism, which is based on John Wesley's theology, and Methodists nowadays have some differences, there are many similarities. For instance°…"

Dad: "Look, no more religion talk. I'm done. Let's go to the place where they have the good-looking waitresses."

This is where I would just roll my eyes, but I would actually be happy that the discussion lasted as long as it did because one of the big problems when we were having a discussion is that he would phrase questions like a statement, walk off proudly like his argument could not be refuted, and then be unwilling to hear a response. This is very problematic because he was not interested in discourse whatsoever; he was only interested in giving his opinion without wanting to hear an argument against it.

It was very frustrating at times. I had solid answers to all of his arguments, but he just did not want to hear them. He was fine with being ignorant. He was very stubborn, not just toward religion, but toward everything. If he did not understand something and had no interest or desire in a topic, he would just tune you out, no matter how important the discussion might be. So when it came to Jesus, an immediate wall went up.

I am sure there are many people that can relate to this type of situation, especially when they became Christians and tried to share their newfound faith with their family or friends. Don't get too upset about this; it happens to most of us. Look at the best example, our role model Jesus. Even His own brothers (brethren) did not believe in Him during His earthly ministry: "For neither did His brethren believe in Him" (John 7:5).

It took Jesus's crucifixion, death, and resurrection from the dead for them to believe. Look at James, who had an encounter with Jesus postresurrection that Paul records in 1 Corinthians 15:7: "After that, he was seen of James; then of all the apostles."

Though he was a skeptic at first, he did become a believer, and James went on to become one of the leaders of the early church. Paul even goes so far as to distinguish him as a "pillar" in his letter to the Galatian Church:

"And when James, Cephas, and John, who seemed to be pillars, perceived the grace°..." (Galatians 2:9).

You see, the problem with us (new believers in this day and age) is that the people who know you the best are the people who knew the old you. They look at the old you and do not know how to take your newfound faith seriously. This does not mean you should give up, but you need to be patient, show them you are for real, and keep planting seeds.

For someone such as my dad, who could not be wrong about anything, it takes time and daily prayer, as frustrating as that may be.

I needed some type of other breakthrough to show him that there was a possibility that he actually could be wrong about something. It would have to be on a subject that had nothing to do with religion, and it would have to be by his own admission.

There were two things that my dad told me that would never happen in life. He worked for a very high-profile investment firm for many years, and he said that a company like that would never go under. Well, it happened in 2008 when the company he worked for over twenty-five years was sold to another company. Then a few weeks later, his 401(k) took a big hit, and he was forced to retire.

He was devastated to say the least. He was sixty-eight years old, and the last thing he wanted to do was look for a new job. He really had no interests outside of work. He was the type of person that lived to work and really did not have any enjoyment outside of his job besides spending time with his family and watching the New York Giants. So when work was taken away from him, and it was not football season, he did not know what to do with himself to keep busy. He was a guy who lived to work and worked to live, and this is very sad, because there is so much more to life than that!

It was also very depressing to see. He was the hardest guy to shop for at holidays. People I knew would buy their dads golf stuff or something to do with a hobby they were interested in, but my dad had none. There were only so many New York Giants and Marine Corps items you can get someone.

His girlfriend who he lived with was not working either, and they were not in love. I do believe at some point they did love each other, but they just grew apart. They did do things together, like go out to dinner to pass time, but they were complete opposites in personality, and they clashed on just about everything. I used to get a kick out of the little things that they argued about. If one of them said it was too hot, you just knew that the other one was too cold. It was that simple. They say that misery loves company; well, they certainly were miserable together, and now they both had more time to spend together being miserable. I really felt bad for the both of them.

Since I was now a Christian and getting really involved in church activities, especially Bible study, I asked my dad to get involved with me, but he did not want anything to do with it.

"If you ever have the chance to preach, I'll come to support you, but other than that, no thank you," he would say.

Me preach? I never in my wildest dreams thought that would ever happen, so he was off the hook there.

He always said, "Church is for old people."

For some reason, he thought he was still a young man.

I studied a lot and was really maturing in the faith. I felt that God was leading me in some direction, but I just did not know where I was going. I spent a lot of time at church around believers and was really enjoying my new life, but I felt that God had something in store for me, and I was trying to prepare myself for what it was.

Then in 2009, the second thing that my dad said would never happen happened. Barack Obama became the first African American to be president of the United States.

Now let me make this clear, my dad was *not* a racist by any measure, but he held fast to his old-school thoughts. He would remind you of a modern-day Archie Bunker with his thought processes as well as his actions. He was the kind of guy who you either loved to be around because he enjoyed being the center of attention, or you just could not stand. There were not many people who could not stand him, but the things he would say were often off the wall and somewhat embarrassing because no matter what it was, he would speak his mind anytime and anywhere. So if there was a cute waitress at a diner, not just would he tell her, but everyone in the place would know about it. I think you can get an idea of what he was like.

So one thing with a guy like this is that they never like to be wrong. I mean no one really does, but when you are filled with pride, and your son says to you, "Hey, Dad, remember those two things you told me that would never happen in life? Well, they both happened. So are you willing to accept the possibility that you can be wrong about some things? How about we talk about Christianity a little bit?"

I then would get a "No, but nice try."

Then not long thereafter, his father got really sick and eventually passed away, leaving his wife, my dad's stepmom behind, who was in her late eighties. They both lived in an old-age home roughly forty-five minutes away. We would go see them maybe every other weekend to spend time with them. They were a beautiful couple to say the least. My dad's real mother died when he was very young around Christmastime, which always made the month of December hard for him. Since my grandfather was in the army, he was stationed overseas, and he met my step-grandmother while he was in Austria. Long story short, they fell in love, got married, and he brought her to the United States when my dad was in his early teens.

My grandpa, or Poppy as I called him, was what many would call a "saver." He just loved to save money in any way that he could and sometimes to the very extreme. We would often get a kick out of going to see him and my step-grandmother, or Gummy as we called her, in the wintertime, and there they would be sitting on the couch, no heat on, watching television, with their winter hats, gloves, and coats on to keep warm. It was actually so cold that you could see their breath when they talked. Then in the summer, in the blistering heat, they'd have all the windows open, not running the air conditioner, sweating profusely just to save money.

Well, it turned out that he sure knew what he was doing, because he was able to save up a substantial amount of money. Although he saved a lot, he never had a chance to spend any of it on something nice for himself, but I am convinced that his enjoyment came from just watching his investments grow. Yes, there are people like that.

Anyhow, since Gummy and my dad were the sole beneficiaries of Poppy's estate, he could not do anything with his investments until Gummy had passed. We began to see Gummy a lot more because she truly had a broken heart, and we did not know how long she could go without her Billy Boy.

I'll never forget the scene at my grandfather's graveside. Since he was a chief warrant officer in the army, he had a military burial. After the officer played "Taps," two soldiers folded the American flag, one walked up to Gummy with the flag, thanked her for his service, said he was sorry for her loss, and then handed her the flag. With tears in her eyes, she just kept saying over and over again, "My Billy Boy is gone." To say that the scene was heartbreaking would be an understatement, and my heart truly went out to her. My dad then said to me, "I want my funeral to be like this."

As time marched on, I was really beginning to get comfortable in the Christian faith. I had such a burning desire to share the gospel with unbelievers. Though I was spending a lot of time at church growing, maturing, and having fellowship with Christians, I was still studying other religions, cults, and now had added to my research early Christianity, theology, the Roman Catholic Church, the vast amounts of Christian denominations, the art of rhetoric (the study of effective speaking, writing, argument styles, and the art of persuasion), and trying to get an understanding of logical fallacies very intensely every day. At this point I still did not know why I felt led to study about some of these subjects. Other Christians I interacted with had no desire to do so and even thought it was kind of strange.

At this point, I did not have to set my alarm anymore. I got out of bed at 4:00 a.m. on my own and ready to study. Why I was doing this, I had no idea, but I felt led to do it. When I told my pastor about this desire, he told me that I should probably back off from studying other things and focus more time on Bible study, because I was still young in the faith, and he did not want to see me get confused or overloaded with information. I could see where he was coming from, but my brain and heart were like a sponge, and I could not stop and get enough.

Then on a Saturday evening in late February 2010, my pastor called me on the phone and sounded very sick. He informed me that he was not feeling good and would not be able to preach the next day. He was calling to ask if I would like to preach in his absence.

I could not believe what I was hearing! I was honored that he put enough faith and trust in me to do so, but I told him that I was very fearful to speak in public, plus what would I preach about? I only had one night to put something together, and I really did not think it would be possible.

He gently stated that he felt led to call me and that God would take care of everything. He wanted me to share my testimony of coming to Christ with the congregation, because although some people knew my story, not everyone did, and it was time for them to know.

I thought about it very quickly, and I felt a push in my heart to say yes. I got off the phone and told my wife, and she was so excited. We got her mother to come over the next day to watch the baby so she could come to hear it. I also called my sisters and my mother to come if they wanted to. Then there was the call that I thought I never would make; I called my dad and said that it was time for him to go to church tomorrow.

He immediately responded, "Are you preaching?"

My response was yes.

He said, "I'll be there."

I did not have too many friends anymore; they were more like bar buddies, and I had given up that scene. I had lost touch with many of them anyway, and my two best friends (my boss and my friend from high school, who was the friend who threw the beer at the guy at the shore) were not Christians, so they would not be interested in coming to hear me preach, especially on such short notice.

I began to pray and asked God to guide me and help me prepare what to say the following day. I also asked for strength to get through it, because I was truly nervous and worried about speaking in public.

Before I knew it, it was the next day. I was getting out of the shower and putting a suit on. I said to myself in the mirror, "Are you really going to do this?"

I felt so nervous, and then my armpits began to sweat. I knew then I was in for a long morning!

My wife and I headed to church, and the parking lot was full. I saw both of my sisters' cars in the parking lot, as well as my mom's, and couldn't believe my eyes because there was my dad pulling up! He kept his word, which he always did. It was not too often he would get out of bed before 1:00 p.m. anymore since he was retired. I was very humbled that everyone made it to hear me and offer support in their own way.

After the morning announcements and some songs of worship, the pastor came forward and addressed the congregation. With a very hoarse voice, he said that he was not feeling good today, and standing in for him to preach would be me.

This is when I felt a bead of sweat drip down from my left armpit and my legs began to shake.

He then said, "Without further ado, Bill, would you please come forward and share with us the message God has placed on your heart? I just know it will be wonderful."

Before I got up, I checked to see if my fly was up for probably the thirtieth time. I stood up and began to walk up front. It seemed like a long walk, but it was probably only about twenty steps. With every step I felt every eye on me. I was a mess, terrified, and just wanted to put my tail between my legs (if I had one) and run in the opposite direction, right out the door, and never come back.

I made my way to the front of the congregation to the pulpit and quietly put my notes and my Bible on the podium. The pastor took off his wireless microphone, attached it to me, put his hand on my shoulder, and said quietly in my ear, "Calm down. I can see you are nervous. You are going to do great! I just know it." His words were very encouraging, and he made his way down to the pew and sat down next to his wife and family. All I had to do was turn the microphone on and then it was go time.

I reached into my pocket, took a deep breath, said a quick prayer, and then turned the microphone on. I looked out over the congregation. To say it was overwhelming would be an understatement. I felt like I was looking out over thirty-five thousand people in a huge auditorium, but in all actuality, there were only about forty-five people in attendance. We were a very small congregation, but this moment for me felt like a Billy Graham crusade. I noticed my dad, who was already sleeping in all his glory with his mouth open, and then my sister gently nudged him to wake him up as she whispered something into his ear. I saw his eyes open, get adjusted, and look at me as if I had not noticed he had been out like a light. I smiled for a moment and then thought, *At least he is here*, as he closed his eyes once again.

I said, "Good morning."

My voice cracked, and I felt like it was noticeably shaky. I thought, *Lord, help me now!*

> Before I came up to the pulpit, all I kept thinking about is what can go wrong while I am up here? My hands became very clammy and wet, while nervousness just entered all over my body! On top of that, my stomach became knotty, I had butterflies, my knees started to tremble, my teeth began to chatter, I felt very cold, sweaty, and then began the negative thoughts and questions: Is my message going to be good enough? Is it going to be long

> enough? I hope I don't stumble on my words. I really hope I don't trip and fall as I walk up there! Is my fly up? Do I have something hanging from my nose? Can you tell that I am not a regular public speaker?

This kind of broke the ice a bit for me as well as the congregation, because it produced a little laughter and made me feel a bit more comfortable. I then felt like something took over, and I was not alone. Only a Christian can describe the feeling—it was a boost of confidence, and I felt energized as if I was filled with the Holy Spirit.

> As you can tell I really am not used to speaking in public; I am not good at it, and in all actuality, I am terrified of even the thought of it. But I must confess that the Bible tells us in Ephesians 6:12, "For our struggle is not against flesh and blood, but against the rulers, against the authorities, against the powers of this dark world and against the spiritual forces of evil°…"

All these thoughts that I share with you I feel derive from Satan, who is trying to suppress me, trying to give me an "I can't" attitude. These are not the thoughts of God, but even though I am a Christian, the battle still wages on. When I finally got up here to the pulpit, I felt a sense of calmness because the battle was won. As I began to speak, I must freely confess that I felt as if I was just filled with the Holy Spirit. I know for a fact that God is with me, and the "I can and I will" attitude is back. Faith is believing that God can and that He will! Praise God! If God is for me, then who can be against me? I am not alone up here. So let me tell you my story.

I then shared my testimony. I preached nonstop for about an hour, and I must say that I never felt more comfortable and more alive in my life. I shared everything from chapter 1 of this book, my life as an unbeliever, and chapter 2 with my experience or testimony bringing me to Jesus through the moral law. I told them about chapter 3 and beginning my life as a believer, and I finally closed with chapter 4, maturing in the faith. The entire congregation got to witness that chapter come to life right before their very eyes each and every week because I was a living example of the power of God and what true change can and will do when you live for Jesus!

The next day, I heard from my pastor, and he said that he really appreciated me filling in for him on such short notice. He just could not tell me how much he appreciated that. He also said that what I did was wonderful, because he felt that I had addressed an issue that was developing in our church that I may not have even known about. He explained to me that this was how the Holy Spirit works sometimes.

I wasn't sure what he was referring to, but he stated that part of my message had convicted some people's hearts, and the right adjustments were made because of what I said.

My pastor also said that overall my presentation was very good. He could tell that I was not a regular public speaker but that I had some great natural talent in the area of communicating. He could also tell that I seemed to lose some of my nervousness after being up there for a few minutes, which I just knew could only be because the Holy Spirit gave me a boldness and confidence like I had never experienced before in my life. He liked how I was straight in what I had to communicate by saying it clearly and in a way that could be easily understood. He jokingly said that he was waiting for me to make some kind of heinous theological slip so he could use his pastoral authority, slap me down, and put me in my place, but I didn't say one thing that he couldn't agree with. My theology was right in line with the scripture and I would make a good Wesleyan. I even did well at using scripture to reinforce my points and I used it correctly, which made him say "bravo" because there were a lot of famous TV preachers who can't seem to do that!

Although I was interrupted by the worship leader toward the end of my sermon, the pastor gave me kudos for handling it in the manner I did. He just raved about how good-natured I was about the whole thing and how I recovered well from it. He also said that the reaction from the congregation was very positive and encouraging, and several members even raved about what I had said. He said that by putting my heart into what I had to say made it very personal and touched all who were there.

Too bad my dad slept through it all.

I mentioned earlier that I had been feeling lately that God had something in store for me, but I was not sure what it could be. The next thing that my pastor told me really spoke to me. He said that he saw clear evidence of God leading me into ministry. If my heart told me that, and it continued to tell me that, I definitely had the gifts and blessings to do it and do it well. After I got a little more practice, he felt that I would polish up very well.

He also said that he was looking forward to seeing more from me and would be looking for opportunities to let me do more. He thanked me for making a low point into a great day for both him and the congregation, and said he was blessed to have me on board.

Talk about encouraging! He really motivated me and got me thinking about ministry. I felt like my entire life I had been sculpted into becoming some type of leader. It all started in the Marine Corps when I became a lance corporal and was put in charge of our platoon, who were all private and private first class ranks. For some reason, leadership just came naturally to me. At my job I was a supervisor giving direction, reprimanding, disciplining when necessary, handling customer service issues and complaints, and dealing with one-on-one mentoring; I not only enjoyed what I did, but I knew I was really good at it.

As soon as I became a Christian, I also began to use biblical leadership and principles to help me as well as employees on a daily basis. Though this was a secular job, and using any type of religious values on the job would not be tolerated, I was able to disguise my beliefs and use them to my advantage. I was the kind of leader that led by example, and who better a role model for me than Jesus?

I began to really pray about ministry and what God could use me for. I sat down with my pastor numerous times and talked about opportunities in the Wesleyan church, and he knew that I was being called into the ministry. He kind of took me under his wing, showed me many aspects of what it took to be a pastor, helped me grow, and discussed the options of becoming a Wesleyan pastor.

Though I was now in my thirties, going to seminary school was not an option. I was a family man, a blue-collar worker, and just did not have the time to devote to school. Plus it would take me many years to get a master's degree going to school part time, but there were ways around it for someone my age in the Wesleyan denomination, which was wonderful. I prayed daily about this and wanted to align my will with God's will, but I felt that becoming a Wesleyan minister was not what God had in mind for me.

So what does a guy in his thirties with a criminal record, a full-time job, a wife, and a daughter do when he feels led into the ministry but does not feel led to do so through his denominational church? There are many other options, and I believe in my heart that the avenue I chose was directed by God's will.

CHAPTER 5

Chaplaincy

A Christian Chaplain

These words are to remind me,
When life doesn't go my way,
I have peace of mind knowing
I will be with Jesus in heaven one day.

Glory and eternal life as promised,
His kingdom set before me.
No more trials and tribulations,
Only in this world I'll see.

Through repentance and godly sorrow,
I know He has mercy on me.
I will do as I am instructed,
Preach the gospel for all to hear and see.

Jesus said He's the only way,
Many refuse to believe or just don't want to hear;
Their eternal destination
Will be torment, fire, and fear.

Please, Lord, give me the strength
To tell the passerby the news.
I do not want anyone to perish;
I don't want one person to lose.

This free gift set forth with
Truth and grace from above
That He sent His only Son to die
Is the greatest gift of love.

So as I look upon these words,
Remind me, Lord, I must do more than pray.
Preach the gospel to all, My son;
Be sure you do this every day.

—Chaplain William H. Schnakenberg IV

I became very confident in my faith. I spoke with boldness and loved to talk about Jesus. There were many Christians who I knew would do everything in their power to avoid such conversations, but I truly looked for opportunities. I think that they avoided conversations because they were worried about possible confrontation or just didn't know how to respond to a hard question. Though I did not have all the answers, I welcomed the opportunity and any type of conversation. Whether it went well or not, I learned from them all. I also just loved to share my testimony with anyone who asked me why I was a Christian. I was studying so much and so many aspects of religions that I was becoming very well-rounded and could hold a conversation with just about anyone about what they believed.

I once was walking down the hallway at work on a late Friday evening when the company was about to close for the day. I worked with a woman who was known to be very set in her ways and sometimes very tough to talk to. As I walked by her office, I peaked in to see what she was doing, and she was packing up her things to head home for the weekend.

I politely stuck my head in and told her to have a good weekend. She wished me the same. I then felt prompted to continue the conversation, and I asked her what she was doing over the weekend.

She said that on Sunday morning she was heading to Trenton with a friend of hers because they liked to volunteer at the soup kitchen. They would help out with making and giving out food to the homeless.

I guess anyone in their right mind would have said, "That is great," but I just felt led to continue a little more, and I asked her why she did it. She proceeded to tell me that she was not sure why she did it, but she guessed because it made her feel good to help out in the community and maybe because it scored some points with God.

I do believe that this was the opportunity I was looking for, because I asked her if she was a Christian, and she politely said that she was not. Now what I said next may seem a bit extreme, but I said, "Huh°...Well, you know that all of your good deeds are like filthy rags in God's eyes, right?"

I smiled, and she looked at me like a deer caught in the headlights. I said, "Oh well, have a great weekend."

I closed the door, and that was the end of the conversation.

I have told many people that story, and they have had many negative things to say about it, but for some reason, I felt led to converse with her like that. I was polite, we were in a secular environment, she brought God up first, and I just knew that the good deeds she thought she was doing were not scoring her any points. I just corrected her way of thinking using God's word and told her to have a great weekend.

Sound harsh? Do you think that a seed was planted? Yes, it was.

That following Monday, she came barging into my office, and she was clearly very upset. I asked her what was wrong, and she proceeded to tell me that she could not get out of her head what I said to her three days ago. She asked me what I meant by it and to show her in the Bible where it said that.

This clearly was evidence of God working. What an opportunity to evangelize, and here we were at work!

I reached down in my bag and pulled out my Bible. I then turned to Isaiah 64:6, where it says, "But we are all as an unclean thing, and all our righteousnesses are as filthy rags; and we all do fade as a leaf; and our iniquities, like the wind, have taken us away."

I let her read it for herself. We had a very fruitful conversation, and from that initial planting, as I call it, we became good friends. We went out and bought her a Bible, and she began reading it. She actually began to come to church and Bible study with me. We even met at each other's houses for personal Bible study. She was so hungry to learn about the Lord! When I came into work early in the morning, it gave me great pleasure to peek into her office and see her reading her Bible. I could see her attitude and behavior changing on a daily basis.

Then, by the grace of God, on March 24, 2010, about a month after I gave my first sermon, while I was at her house going over the Sermon on the Mount, she said she was ready to become a Christian. God used me that day, and I led her to Christ. She had goosebumps all over her arms, and it was an amazing experience. I left her house knowing that I was being called into the ministry, but I did not know where to turn. A month later, on April 28, she was baptized by my pastor at my church, and it was awesome to say the least.

I was starting to see that when God places something on your heart, you have a choice—either to act on it or not. I am so glad that I said something that day, and who would have thought it would have been done like that? It was very bold, and I took a chance on some negative feedback, but I jumped on the opportunity to do so, and more importantly I felt led. Now I highly recommend that you do not just start telling people that all of their good deeds are like filthy rags. We must always listen to the Holy Spirit, and given the correct opportunity to do so, He will place on your heart what and when to say something. In this instance, it worked only because I felt led to do so.

As I was searching out ministry opportunities outside of the Wesleyan church, my pastor began to give me more opportunities to preach in his absence. Over time, I began to really get comfortable, and I felt at home at the pulpit. It was like a second office for me. I started a men's Bible study at the church, and it really took off. I was very involved doing elder responsibilities and board meetings at church, but I still devoted much time to my family, personal study (now I added studying arguments for and against Christianity,) and looking into other ministry opportunities.

I was somewhat caught between a rock and a hard place though. Everywhere I looked within Christian organizations and secular institutions to become a Christian leader, one must have at least a master of divinity degree. Now there I was in my thirties with a full-time job and a family, and I did not have the time or the money to devote to a college degree. Given my blue-collar income, especially with the pay cut I had just taken, I was not prepared to have added expenses or find the time to devote to a college education.

The only thing going for me was that I had a zeal to serve the Lord, become a leader, studied a lot in my free time, and really felt a calling. But everywhere I went, it just seemed like a dead end. Then after much prayer, my prayers were finally answered.

In the course of my personal study, I researched the early church and traditions that had come to pass throughout history. There was a legend of a man named Martin of Tours who was a soldier of the fourth century. As the legend goes, he was met on a cold winter's night at one of the gates of the French city of Amiens by a beggar crying for alms. Martin reached into his purse and found it empty. Touched with compassion, he took off his heavy cloak and, with his sword, slashed it in two, giving half to the beggar and keeping the other half for himself. That night, Jesus appeared to Martin in a dream wearing the cloak and said, "What thou hast done for the poor man, thou hast done for Me."

Martin was so moved by the vision that he sought baptism and later abandoned his military career to devote himself to being a Christian. He dedicated his life to Christianity. He was zealous in making converts to the church. In time Martin became the patron saint of France, and his cloak, considered a sacred relic, was often carried into battle by French kings.

The officer appointed to watch over the sacred cloak (in Latin: *cappa* or *capella*) was known in French as the *chapelain,* from which the English word chaplain derives. There have been countless stories regarding this legend as well as beautiful art dedicated to the famous scene of Martin slashing his cloak in half. One painting by an unknown Hungarian in 1490 and a painting by El Greco in the mid-fifteen to early sixteen hundreds are just breathtaking.

With this beautiful introduction to the word *chaplain*, I felt moved to look into what chaplaincy was and is to the modern mind. I had heard of the word before, but I had no idea what it meant. When I was in the Marine Corps, we had chaplains of all religious faiths on Parris Island and Camp Lejeune, but I never felt the need to see one.

The word *chaplain* has Christian roots, but nowadays there are many types of chaplains that are not Christian. Often, a chaplain is considered someone who is a representative of a religious tradition that is tied to a secular institution. This could range from the military to schools and hospitals as well as law enforcement and so on. There is deep-rooted history associated with the word *chaplain* in the Christian world, and often early Christian chaplains were in charge of private Christian chapels or in charge of leading private fellowship.

All chaplains have different types of training, but more often than not, it is a job description that does not offer much pay. Although I was not looking to make a lot of money, I did need to do something that could compensate what I was making now or find something that I could do part time, or my dream would be at my own leisure.

After countless hours of investigating chaplaincy, I felt led to apply to an accredited institution that I read about and was spoken of very highly. I spoke with the president of the organization, and after a detailed background check on me, obviously questions were brought up. I explained how I was a changed man and was now living for the Lord and trying to answer my calling. After a period of intense study and testing in the areas of biblical study (Old and New Testament), disaster response, cultural diversity and sensitivity, public safety chaplaincy, hospice care ministry, prison ministry, nursing home ministry, pastoral crisis counseling, evangelism, intercessory prayer, and domestic violence, I was ordained as a nondenominational chaplain on July 29, 2010.

Though I was excited about it, I could not believe that just the day before the Parx Casino opened up about ten miles away from where my dad lived! I just knew when he found out about it, it was going to be bad news because he would not have to drive to Atlantic City anymore; he could just drive right down the road to gamble.

My life in chaplaincy and in the ministry had begun, a role that I was going to take very seriously, but I did not know where the Lord was going to take me from there. Though I was now an ordained nondenominational chaplain, it was up to me, and more importantly to God's guidance, what I was going to do as a chaplain.

After I explained what I had done to my pastor, he had mixed emotions about it. I know that he really wanted me to become a Wesleyan pastor, but I just could not do it, feeling that the Lord was not behind the decision. He respected my position and still somewhat took me under his wing with responsibilities at church.

I did not tell too many people about becoming a chaplain, only because I did not know what I was going to do next. I did tell my wife, family, and two closest friends. After a lengthy conversation with the one who threw that beer can at that guy several years back, I must truly say that he was happy for me and the change in my life. He said that I had made a complete 180 degree turn, and he was proud of me. Although he was raised as a Roman Catholic growing up, he had not been to church in quite a while, and he said that he had some issues and questions about the faith because he lost his dad when he was so young. He also told me that he was going to ask his girlfriend to marry him, and they would be honored if I could marry them.

I thought to myself, *Me officiate a wedding? Well, I can do it; I just don't know the logistics of how to do it.*

After countless hours of investigating, I knew that I could do it, and I gladly consented to officiate my first wedding. I sat down with my friend and his fiancée on numerous occasions to explain what marriage meant in God's eyes. It was my first time premarriage counseling, and I loved every minute of it. I also put together my first wedding ceremony, and on October 29⁰ 2010, I officiated my first wedding. It truly was an awesome honor.

People just raved about it and could not believe it was the first time I had done one. I did not charge them a dime; it was my gift to them for their wedding. As I investigated, I could not believe how much some officiants were charging! The fee ranged from one hundred to five hundred dollars, and some I even saw charge up to a thousand dollars or even more!

I then felt it was time to begin a Christian ministry. I decided to take it slow by creating a website, which was a lot of fun, and to get involved in social networking and media. I did not know the first thing about setting anything up on social media and sent many messages to sites asking for help. All of them turned me down unless I gave them money. Finally I reached out to a certain site asking for help, and I got a response from someone.

He and I became really great friends. He actually was the first person I ever spoke to who had experienced a miracle. When he was a kid, he was legally blind. His parents took him to church, a Wesleyan church in fact, the elders laid hands on him, and his sight was restored. From there on out he was a believer. He showed me the ropes in social media, and I thank God that He led me to him.

All I needed to do now was to come up with a ministry name. My favorite verse in the Bible is Romans 8:28, which says, "And we know that all things work together for good to them that love God, to them who are the called according to His purpose."

I felt led to use this somehow in the ministry name. So after much prayer, along with another Christian brother of mine who I met through social media and lived in Texas, I decided to call the ministry Beloved 8:28.

We named it Beloved 8:28 because this scripture is not only a great verse, but it may just be one of the most important scriptures in the entire Bible. We just knew that in a lost and dying world it is very hard sometimes to see a light at the end of the tunnel or to believe that something good could ever come out of a bad situation.

This is where this scripture applies best. It applies to all Christians in any situation. Those who are Christ's (Christians) are honored with these privileges (all things God works for the good). Even though we belong to Christ, we will still face afflictions, trials, and tribulations. Even though we pray and the Spirit makes intercession for us, our own personal troubles will still continue.

It is not the case that the Spirit's intercession is not working on our behalf, but we can know that all this is working together for our good.

As God has and always will love us, we in return love God. Where there is love, there is trust, where there is trust, there is hope, where there is hope, there is faith, and where there is faith, there is peace. No one will ever know true peace until they come to know Jesus. This was our mission in the ministry.

Once you come to know Jesus, your soul's affection toward God will be the chief good and highest end. It is our love of God that makes every situation sweet and therefore profitable. Those who love God make the best of all He does and take it all in good part, in any situation life may throw at them whether good or bad.

As Christians we are called according to an eternal purpose. The call is effectual, not according to any merit or desire of ours, but according to God's own gracious purpose. We are pilgrims while we walk the Earth waiting to go to our eternal home prepared for us.

All that God performs He performs for us. Though we may not understand it at the time of our trials, we must learn to trust Him. Either directly or indirectly, every trial we undergo is for the spiritual good of those who love God, breaking them off from sin, bringing them nearer to God, weaning them from the world and its fading pleasures, and fitting them for heaven.

This was the hope we were trying to encourage in believers and offer to unbelievers. It truly was a blessing, and Beloved 8:28 had over ten thousand followers on social media from all over the world within four months! We were helping and meeting many people, and we were blessed by what God was doing in our lives and theirs.

I then started to go to yard sales and buy Bibles. The reason I did this was because some people that I was interacting with did not have a Bible and some could not afford one. Some lived here in the States and others overseas. I really thought that it was necessary that every Christian should have one. If I could pick up a Bible for a quarter and have other people do the same, we could get Bibles to all who needed one. At some yard sales, there would be ten to fifteen Bibles for sale, and often the people selling them gave them to me for free after I told them what I was trying to do.

I also put the word out on social media that if anyone had any extra Bibles we would take them and get them to someone who needed one. I would even take care of shipping, and regardless of their condition, we would take them all. Though they were used, I truly loved what Charles Spurgeon (1834–1892) who was known as the Prince of

Preachers, said: "A Bible that's falling apart usually belongs to someone who isn't."

Well, let's get that used Bible to someone who needs one!

The program took off, and one of the biggest honors was getting twenty Bibles to a women's Bible study in Houston, Texas. The woman who contacted me was so grateful when she received them. It was nice to see this idea working.

The ministry was taking off, and we were loving every minute of it. We also had our fair share of opposition, but we took it in good stride. We were humble and defended the faith, and we learned a lot about unbelievers who did not want to hear the message but just wanted to mock, ridicule, and cause problems. This comes with the territory, and it only deepened our faith. The ministry began to grow, and I reached out to other Christians to help where I felt we needed it.

In this process, the Christian that showed me the ropes on social media reached out to me and asked if I could help him with his ministry as well. He had a page with over 1.5 million subscribers. He asked if I could help out with answering messages because there were just too many. He had other Christians helping out, but they just could not keep up.

Between helping people out on my page and his page, I was very busy in the cyber world. I never would have thought there would be so much work to be done in cyberspace. We were helping people from all over the world tackle issues that they were experiencing on their walk as Christians. I think it made them feel more comfortable to talk with someone anonymous who they would never see. They came for advice, and I truly worked alongside many gifted Christians giving remarkable and godly advice. Any type of problem that you can think of, it was there. It ranged from simple prayer requests to battling depression and even talking people out of the thoughts of suicide.

We also received many forms of opposition from all sorts of people in various religions and faiths, including agnosticism and atheism. I learned how to debate people in a friendly but bold and polite manner. Discussions varied depending on who you were talking with, but from all the studying that I was doing, I was familiar with how to defend the faith quite well and using opposing religious weaknesses against the person trying to discredit Christianity. Many were ignorant of their own beliefs, some were just looking to pick a fight, and some would even attack me, which is known as an ***ad hominem*** logical fallacy derived from Latin for "to the man" or "to the person," which means rather than attacking the argument directly they attacked me personally. Some also used profanity and vulgar language, and most of them, when they felt they were not winning the argument that they started, we would never hear from them again.

I was also seeing a lot of sincere curiosity within the cyber world. People would send messages sincerely seeking answers, and we were there to help. They were lost, and the Lord used us to lead them to the light. I was at the point where the Lord would use me to bring someone to Jesus daily, sometimes even more than one person a day! It was amazing, and I had no idea that chaplaincy would take me into the cyber world first, but then I realized that the Lord had more in store for me than just the cyber world.

CHAPTER 6

Blue-Collar Faith

Life in the cyber world was certainly keeping me very busy. I spent a lot of my time on the computer. I never thought I would spend so much time doing so, but at the time it really felt as if that was where I was needed.

My wife did not understand it at all at first, but then I began sharing some messages with her. She could not believe some of the things she was reading! Most of the messages I shared with her were from people just pouring their hearts out and needing somewhere to turn for advice. The debates I was having with other people was beyond her understanding because she did not really get too into religious disputes; however, I loved it. I was learning a lot about myself and getting even stronger in my faith seeing how weak a lot of people's arguments were against Christianity or how their misunderstandings totally misconstrued their overall outlook on life.

Every chance I had, I would be answering some type of message. It truly was a tremendous responsibility. If I saw there were twenty unread messages and did not have the time to address them, I would reach out to the other Christians on the ministry team to see if they had some time to answer them. We worked very well together, and we were from all over the country. If someone did not feel comfortable with answering a certain message, we began to get a good idea who would be the best suited to help depending on what the message was. It turned out that all debate format messages were directed to me. Most of them were from atheists, agnostics, Muslims, and Mormons. Some were really fruitful discussions, and others were there just to cause trouble. Either way, I was ready. It got to the point where it seemed like it was the same argument over and over again, so I kept a folder and just copied and pasted my response so I did not have to take the time to type it out anymore.

I always made sure that I put my daily reading of the Bible, studying other books, and my family first before I logged onto the computer, so there was a healthy balance.

Even at my secular job, when there was downtime, I devoted it to studying. I was a supervisor, so I always made sure all the work was done first before I did anything personal because I truly believed in leading by example.

One day I was in my office finishing up some paperwork at my desk. Our department was in the basement of a large building near a loading dock.

My employees were doing their normal routine when suddenly there was a loud noise.

As I put my pen down and jumped out of my seat to see what the noise was, one of my employees ran into my office and frantically said, "Come here quick! He fell down and is bleeding!"

I hurried as fast as I could to assess the situation.

There in front of me lay a six foot, three inch 250 pound man bleeding from his head, ears, foaming from his mouth, going into convulsions, and murmuring things that we could not understand.

The two other employees and I stood and watched the scene in horror.

We all began to panic, but I immediately told the one employee to call 911 and the other one to call our in-house security department.

We had phones in the room we were in, but they both ran out of the room!

Why they left, I do not know, but now I am coming to realize that this moment I was about to witness God only intended for me to see.

As I stood there alone, the big man got to his knees and began very violently hitting his head against the floor.

I yelled his name and told him to stop, but there was no use because he was in some type of seizure!

I jumped onto his back, wrapped my legs around his waist, and put my arms around his neck (a rear naked choke from mixed martial arts that I learned, but I did not apply pressure around his neck to choke him). I then pulled him down to his side to stop him from hitting his head against the concrete floor.

He was literally twice my size, but I finally managed to fully pull him to the side.

His body then went limp in my arms, and my one leg was trapped between the floor and his side. His lifeless body was extremely heavy, and then my worst fears came true.

His high energy breathing began to slow down, and he stopped breathing altogether.

I was able to pull my leg out from underneath of him, and I carefully crawled out and kneeled before him.

I was nervous, I was shaken, and my adrenaline was pumping. I looked at his mouth, and it was open with blood and white foam trickling out of the side of it. I put my finger close to his nose and mouth to see if I could feel air coming out of it, and there was none. I put my hand on his chest, and I could not feel a heartbeat.

I had learned CPR in the Marine Corps, and I was really grappling with the idea of giving him mouth-to-mouth seeing all the white foam and blood.

It was all happening so fast, and I did the only thing I could think of to do, hoping paramedics or the police would be running through the door any second.

I closed my eyes and began to pray.

What I said, I have no idea. All I knew is that I needed strength, I needed help, and I reached out to my Lord and Savior.

All I remember is closing the prayer in Jesus's name.

At that very moment, I opened my eyes, and as God as my witness, the lifeless body before me gasped for air.

It seemed that his breathing was now controlled; he lay there peacefully and was not going into seizures like before.

I stood up in awe, amazement, shock, and praised God for what I had just witnessed.

People began to flood into the room from all the entry points in the department—employees, police, paramedics, and all kinds of people ready to help.

They helped him onto a stretcher, and as he was coming to, they began to ask him questions, but he did not remember anything. The two employees that had witnessed the fall told the police that he was sitting at his desk typing, and then all of sudden, out of nowhere, he just pushed his seat back and went full force forward out of his chair headfirst onto the concrete floor. They then ran and got me, and I in turn told them to call the police and get security.

Everyone had missed this miracle and or answered prayer, but I know it was intended only for me to experience and witness. This just further confirmed my faith in Christ and how prayers are still answered.

I shared this experience with my boss, who was my good friend and had his doubts about Christianity, and it really got him thinking.

To this day, I don't know what I said in the very personal prayer, but the prayer confirmed two Scriptural truths for me.

What Paul said in Romans 8:26: "Likewise the Spirit also helpeth our infirmities: for we know not what we should pray for as we ought: but the Spirit itself maketh intercession for us with groanings which cannot be uttered"; And what Jesus said in John 14:12–14: "Verily, verily, I say unto you, He that believeth on me, the works that I do shall he do also; and greater works than these shall he do; because I go unto my Father. And whatsoever ye shall ask in my name, that will I do, that the Father may be glorified in the Son. If ye shall ask any thing in my name, I will do it."

The man that got injured that day was in the hospital for a few days being evaluated and then finally came home. He took off work for about a week to recuperate. The entire time he was out, I could not stop thinking about what had happened. I also really felt in my heart I should tell him what I had experienced, but I did not want to cross the line as his supervisor in a secular environment with a religious conversation.

I was at odds, but I then felt led and decided to give him a telephone call to tell him what happened. It was about a five-minute conversation, and he already knew that I was a Christian. I told him that I knew that he was not, but I would like to tell him what had happened. I told him that it was a faith matter, and if he did not want to hear it, I would not tell him, but he told me it was okay.

I got straight to the point, and I said I did not know where he stood with his belief in God or with the power of prayer being answered, but I told him in great detail what I experienced with him that day.

He seemed in shock and there was no response for a few seconds. I said that if he ever wanted to talk about it off the record and not at work, I would be more than happy to talk to him more about Jesus, my Lord and Savior, who could be his Lord and Savior as well. He thanked me for sharing with him our experience.

He came back to work the following week, and it was business as usual. I never brought it up again, and let the ball be in his court if he wanted to talk.

He never did.

Not to jump the gun, because I am trying to keep everything I write in this book in chronological order, but I do think that it is important to skip ahead for a moment to about four years later. This gentleman was still working with me, and he was scheduled to come in one day, but he was what we call a "no call, no show."

This was very odd for him because he would come in late only once in a while, always scheduled days off, and if he was sick, he would definitely call out that day or the day prior.

We tried to call him on his cell phone all day long, but there was no response.

Around five o'clock on that very day, we received a call from his brother telling us that he and his mother had found him dead on the kitchen floor. He had a heart attack at the age of thirty-six.

It was very tragic and depressing within our workforce to lose someone who was so young, but death has a strange way of putting life into perspective sometimes.

Now I'm going to get back into writing about four years prior to his death …

My dad now really was not doing much with his time. I was actually thankful for his girlfriend. Though they did not get along very well, she kept him going and did her best to keep him motivated. If it not for her, it would be highly unlikely he would be seeing the doctor on a regular basis, taking his medication, or even just waking up at a decent hour. She was actually someone who did a lot with her time and kept herself busy. She was even a Christian and very active at her church. She also exercised, loved to walk, and would travel a lot to see her daughters and grandchildren who lived in New York. I must say that she was very motivated, enjoyed being retired, and she really tried to get my dad involved in something, but every attempt was a failure.

My dad did not exercise, but at least when he had a full-time job, he walked around. He did not have a good diet, and he drank alcohol almost daily. It was not that he was a drunk, but he would have a few drinks at dinner and a couple of nightcaps as he called them. They usually involved hard liquor, such as his favorite Grand Marnier (very high in sugar), Bloody Mary (high in salt), and scotch or rum and diet soda (also high in sugar).

Now his days basically consisted of sleeping until about one in the afternoon, even though his girlfriend started the process of trying to wake him up around ten. He then would finally get up, very aggravated and not pleasant to be around, go downstairs, eat a bowl of cereal, drink some coffee, watch television for a little while, and then it was time for an afternoon nap until about four or five o'clock. Then he and his girlfriend would go out together for dinner or she would cook something somewhat nutritious, and then he would take another nap, wake up around nine or ten o'clock, watch television, and then close the night out by checking funny forwards in his e-mail or playing solitaire on the computer.

This was not a good lifestyle for anyone, especially someone in their late sixties to early seventies. He was hard of hearing in his right ear and had a hearing aid, but he did not want to wear it because he thought it made him look old. He also had high blood pressure, diabetes for which he took insulin, gout, vascular disease, high cholesterol, thyroid issues, had two strokes in the past, suffered from depression, and he smoked now easily two packs of cigarettes a day. Sooner or later I just knew something bad was going to happen.

I stopped by his house one day after work, and he told me that he had a doctor's appointment that day. It was about getting test results back, and he now had to schedule to go to the hospital and have surgery. The doctor said that he had squamous cell cancer in his neck, and they had to remove some lymph nodes.

This was the first time I actually saw my dad scared about anything in his life. He did not like hospitals or even a dentist's chair. He once got a tooth pulled and the dentist did not give him enough novocaine. He felt some pain, screamed, got out of the chair, punched the dentist, and knocked him out.

No one likes pain, but he hated even the very thought of it. When you start throwing around a word like *cancer*, it really strikes fear into your soul, and my dad was scared to death.

I wanted to jump on this opportunity to talk to him about Jesus, but I needed to be careful because I knew that his emotions were running high. I mean mine were too; I had just found out that my dad had cancer, and I was more concerned about his salvation. In my mind, I had a lot to do to stimulate his mind to think about Christianity, but it was up to the Holy Spirit to open his heart.

The conversation went something like this:

Me: "Dad, tell me exactly why you are scared. Is it because you are scared to die?"

Dad: "Yes, of course it is. I don't want to die. I'm not ready to die. Everyone is scared to die, aren't you? Oh, wait, you are a priest now, so I guess you're not."

Me: "Dad, I'm not a priest. I think everyone has a natural fear of the dying process for different reasons. Whether it is the fear of being dead, the actual dying process, or just the fear of the unknown°..."

Dad: "No one knows what will happen when you die."

Me: "Well, we do know that it is the truth about life, and we should all take the time to think about it. I mean this is one of the many points that made me become a Christian."

Dad: "So, just because you are a Christian, you are not scared to die?"

Me: "If I answered no, I would be lying, but it is only one kind of fear. The only fear that I have is the momentary physical act of death. I think that everyone naturally has that fear whether you are a Christian or not. No one knows for certain exactly what it physically feels like to die."

Dad: "That is all you are scared of?"

Me: "Honestly, yes it is. This is my only fear, but I know it will only be for a moment. A moment everyone has gone through that has died or will go through when they die. And, when that moment is over, it is over."

Dad: "Yeah, true, but it is scary to think about."

Me: "Yeah, but if you really think about it, a moment is such a tiny portion of time. It is only an instant, and such a brief period of time compared to our time here on earth and eternity. I do believe people dwell fearfully on this brief moment way too much, especially being a Christian."

Dad: "Yeah, uh huh, and why is that?"

Me: "Because as a Christian, we are to always be confident, knowing that while we are at home in the body, we are absent from the Lord, and we should be confident and willing, rather, to be absent from the body and be present with the Lord.'

Dad: "Oh, really, I guess your Bible says that?"

Me: "Yes, it does. I was paraphrasing a scripture. Did you notice how I said the word *confident* twice?"(I was referencing 2 Corinthians 5:6–8: "Therefore we are always confident, knowing that, whilst we are at home in the body, we are absent from the Lord: (For we walk by faith, not by sight:) We are confident, I say, and willing rather to be absent from the body, and to be present with the Lord.")

Dad: "Yeah, whatever."

Me: "Dad, I can tell I am losing you here, but to be confident is a pretty powerful word, and Paul used it twice! Being confident is being full of conviction and having and or showing assurance. This is very encouraging! This is why I don't have to focus on the dying moment, because it will be so quick, and then after that, I can have confidence knowing that I will be with Jesus after I die. It is actually by God's grace that He lets me die, so I can then go on to°..."

Dad: "Okay, hold up, I really don't feel like talking about this anymore. I am going to call and schedule the surgery, and°..."

Me: "Dad, the way doctors are able to treat cancer nowadays is unbelievable. I really don't think you have much to worry about. They will just put you under, do the surgery, and then you will be on your way. I'm sure then there will be radiation treatments and°..."

Dad: "I just hope that I wake up."

Me: "Me too. I'll be there; I'm sure all your kids will be there offering you support."

Dad: "All right, I'm sure you have to get going home to the wife and the baby."

Me: "Yeah, but before I go, do you mind if I pray for you?"

This was the first time in my life I ever asked my dad this. I was very hesitant doing so because I was not sure how he was going to react. He looked like he was in heavy thought for a few seconds, looked around the room, and then looked directly at me, and said, "You know what? Go right ahead; I would like that."

Then, on the late afternoon of December 14, 2010, right there in his living room, sitting on his couch, I prayed for my father in front of him for the very first time. I prayed for his salvation and for the Lord to open his stubborn heart daily in my own personal prayer time, but this moment really meant a lot to me. I prayed that though my dad had lived a life far from God, I asked that this fearful experience for my dad help to begin a relationship with Jesus Christ. I prayed that he would be made well, and his health would get better. I asked God to step in with divine intervention, and when he went under anesthesia, for God to keep him safe and from harm. I prayed for God to bless and accompany my dad, to guide him in all that he did from there on out, to direct him with the Holy Spirit in all of his ways, and to have him make a full, healthy, painless recovery. I prayed that God be with my dad because his own strength would not be enough; he would need God's strength to get him through this time. I asked that everything be a complete success in Jesus's name. When I was finished, my dad actually even said, "Thank you."

Weeks then went by and the surgery finally happened. The operation went all according to schedule. My dad woke up, so he was extremely happy about that. The doctors removed twenty-four lymph nodes from the left side of his neck, and only one tested positive for cancer. Due to the impact of the surgery, it made the side of his face collapse a little bit.

He also lost feeling in part of his tongue and his taste buds were affected.

The experience gave him a scare, and he asked his family doctor, who he was very close with, what he could do to live longer. He loved his doctor, and it seemed like he was the only guy he would actually follow through on taking advice from. His doctor told him to quit smoking, and you know what? He quit. I just wish his doctor was a Christian and told him about the gospel!

He also made other changes in his diet and even began to walk a little more. With these little changes he made in his lifestyle, you certainly could see a difference.

A couple of months later he had a recurrence in a lymph node that tested positive for cancer. He was treated with radiation, and after thirty-five treatments, he was cancer free. We were not sure if this was going to be a common occurrence, but we had to take it day by day. Besides a minor staph infection in his right calf, things were okay with his health for a while.

CHAPTER 7

Apologetics

The year of 2012 started off with a bang for my family because we found out that my wife was expecting our second child. We were so excited! Our daughter was extremely happy and could not wait to have a brother or sister to play with.

I also started to do more weddings, and I made it mandatory to sit down with the couple to explain how important counseling was in preparation for marriage. I always used biblical principles, and everyone seemed so enlightened and got a lot out of the few sessions I required. I did not really charge anything and people rarely tipped, but I was there more to gain the experience. The greatest enjoyment for me though was writing the ceremony. Not one ceremony that I put together was the same. Each and every one of them was unique, pertaining to a theme that a particular couple may have had, or how they met, and so on.

I was traveling all over Pennsylvania, New Jersey, Delaware, and even Maryland doing ceremonies at locations that ranged from million-dollar places to the backroom of a hotdog stand on a Little League baseball field in a rough part of a city. I met a lot of very interesting people, and I was quite surprised how many Christians I was meeting who did not have a home church. I did my best to encourage them to find one, but after the wedding, my work was done unless they contacted me again for some type of spiritual assistance, which often happened, and I was always there for people who needed me.

I did not realize how much work it was for me if there was not a professional wedding coordinator at the venue! I was wet behind the ears doing these duties, and I sincerely thanked God that my pastor let me observe the way he did weddings at our church.

He showed me the ropes, his style, and how to deal with hard-headed family and friends that wanted to be in charge, as well as how to handle a groomzilla or bridezilla. Yes, even the groom can be a "zilla" even more than you may think! It is very stressful to handle situations when you have five to ten people barking orders at the same time, and you always have just one person who is way out of control who needs to be put in his or her place. That is where you step in—in a loving, polite way, of course.

My pastor said that I must always remember that I am there to make the day glorify God, as beautiful as possible, and unforgettable for the bride and groom, but there must be only one person in charge at all times, and I was the person. I really learned a lot from him and thank him from the bottom of my heart for always taking the time to help me in any way that I needed.

At the time I was new at officiating wedding ceremonies, I still had to figure out my own style, and I knew that I had to be patient and it would come in time.

I was a nervous wreck for the first wedding that I had to do without a wedding coordinator. I was at this particular wedding rehearsal, and one of the groomsmen was an atheist.

I was aware of this because the groom gave me a heads up that he might say something derogatory about Christianity and not to take it personally. I told him that it was not a big deal, but I thanked him for letting me know.

I was running around like a chicken with its head cut off, and this is when the gentleman decided to make his move to let me know his stance on his beliefs. He and I, as well as the other groomsmen and the best man, were standing in the spot where the bride and groom were going to exchange their vows.

He said, without looking at me, with much sarcasm in his voice, "I really don't understand why people believe there is a God when science has disproved the need for a God time and time again."

I watched as the best man and groomsmen just looked at each other and seemed to be a bit uncomfortable about what he said.

I knew that I would not have much time to address this because I still had a lot to do, but I reluctantly said, "You know, I really wish I had the time to discuss this, but right now, I kind of have my hands full; but quickly, I am very curious, tell me, just give me one example on how science has disproved the need for God time and time again?"

He said, "Well, look at the big bang theory. With that, you do not need a Creator."

I said, "Really? That is interesting. I respectfully disagree with you, because I do believe in a big bang theory too, which points to the need for a Creator."

He said, "That is just a preposterous statement! You cannot have both! You are contradicting yourself! You cannot believe in both! That does not make any sense," with a laugh.

I said, "Believe it or not, it makes perfect sense. 'In the beginning, God created'; with these five words, the universe came into existence and time therefore began. This is where the true big bang happened, so there is no contradiction."

I looked over at the best man and groomsmen, and they were really paying attention to this conversation. I also looked over to where the bride and groom were going to need me next, and they were clearly not ready for me to come over yet.

He said, "So at that moment time began, huh? Who are you to say that even time began? I think time never had a beginning and the universe has always been infinite."

He looked over at the best man and the groomsmen and nodded his head with pride. I could tell they were anxiously waiting to see what I was going to say next. I realized that this conversation may not be intended for the atheist. His mind may have already been made up, so there was no way to persuade him to think otherwise, but that may not be the case for the people who were overhearing our conversation.

I said, "Okay, so according to your logic, let me try to understand this. Can we agree that if we were to define infinite, we are saying it means endless, or like a number that just keeps going on forever?"

He said, "Yup. In mathematics it is immeasurable because it goes on and on and on, and there just is no end. You don't have to be a rocket scientist to figure that out."

I felt as if he were trying to insult my intelligence. He was obviously well educated, but that did not mean his argument was correct. I figured I'd play his little game and be a bit sarcastic as well. Nothing wrong with enforcing your points with a little sarcasm sometimes.

I said, "Okay, good. So here is my question for you. If there were an infinite amount of days before today, then how is today even here? Today would have never arrived, and I would say today would have never arrived yet, but I can't because it never would."

He said, "What do you mean? That does not make any sense."

I said, "Well, if the universe is infinite, and time never had a beginning, it then was always infinite, so how did today arrive? Now I am not a rocket scientist, but I do see a problem with that. Do you?"

I took a look at the groomsmen and best man, and by the looks on their faces, it appeared as though they seemed a bit gratified about what I said. A couple of them were actually chuckling a little bit. The guy I was speaking to seemed a bit agitated and frustrated, so I decided to press my point a little further.

I said, "So logically, there must have been a finite, number of days before today, or we would have never arrived at today, yesterday, or even tomorrow for the sake of the argument. Therefore, time had a beginning, and if there is a beginning, there must be something or someone to make that start, and that in my opinion points to a Creator, unless you have another theory?"

I then was being summoned from across the way to help out and excused myself. I walked away and went back to coordinating the wedding. When I had some free time, I went over to the atheist again, asked if he thought about what I had said, and he said he did not want to talk about it anymore. In my opinion, at least a seed was planted, not only for him, but for the others that had overheard our conversation. Conversations like that I really enjoyed.

A couple of weeks later, my youngest sister had a situation where she needed some help, so I took the day off of work, and I took her to the doctor. She was going to be there most of the day, and I could not be there with her, and I did not want to sit in the waiting room, so I decided to go for a ride.

I did not know where I was going, and I was not familiar with the area I was in, but I knew that I was hungry. The first place I saw was a bar. I had not been inside of a bar in a long time, and the last time I left one, I know I was pretty drunk. I thought to myself, *Wow, I really have changed a lot.*

I walked in and grabbed a bar stool and a menu. There was no one at the bar, and the restaurant part was pretty empty. The bartender asked me if I would like a drink. I thought, *Why not?* So I ordered a pint of Guinness, which was my favorite beer that I had not had in a really long time, and I then ordered some food.

An older woman then walked in and sat on a bar stool two down from me. It was a very dark bar, there was not much going on, and I decided to engage in a conversation with her after she got a drink. There was a big difference now in engaging in a conversation with a woman at a bar for me than ten years ago. Ten years ago, I would have had ulterior motives on my mind, mostly how to try and get this woman to come home with me, but now I was married, and all I could think about was, *Does this woman know Jesus as her Lord and Savior?* I really did a complete 180 degree turn in life thinking like this!

So I sparked up a quick, friendly line by asking how she was doing today. I wanted to see if she was up for talking to a complete stranger, and I knew I would be able to get a good vibe by the way she responded. She politely said that she was doing well, and in turn she asked me how I was doing.

This gave me the in for further engagement, and I told her I was doing awesome, and I could not believe I was in a bar! I told her that I had not been in a bar for years, and that this was the first drink I had had in a long time.

She then responded with wanting to know more, so I decided to tell her my story if she was up for hearing it. She said that she would love to.

It's not that I like talking about myself, but I wanted to see how open she was to a spiritual conversation. I asked her if she was a Christian, and she said that she was not and that she was actually Jewish.

I thought to myself, *Jackpot! I have never had a conversation in person with a Jewish person before. This could get very interesting.*

I told her to keep an open mind because I was about to tell her how I became a Christian. She said that she was very curious to hear my story.

I talked nonstop for about a half hour while she carefully and intently listened to every word I had to say. When I was finished, she asked all kinds of great questions, which I was more than prepared for.

I then had some questions for her. I asked her if she was acquainted with the Old Testament, which I figured she was, because she was Jewish, and if she ever knew about the messianic prophecies foretold in them and how Jesus fulfilled them.

She said that she did not. She was very surprised by what I said, and asked if I could name just one. She said that she was not really well versed in the Old Testament, and not all Jewish people were. Some were, but not all of them.

The only one that I could think of offhand was the suffering servant from Isaiah 53. I did not know it by heart, it was rather long, but I knew that I had a Bible out in the car. I told her to sit tight and that I would be right back.

I ran out to my car, got it, and brought it back in. I turned to Isaiah 53 and read it out loud.

> Who hath believed our report? And to whom is the arm of the LORD revealed? For He shall grow up before him as a tender plant, and as a root out of a dry ground: He hath no form nor comeliness; and when we shall see Him, there is no beauty that we should desire Him. He is despised and rejected of men; a man of sorrows, and acquainted with grief: and we hid as it were our faces from Him; He was despised, and we esteemed Him not. Surely He hath borne our griefs, and carried our sorrows: yet we did esteem Him stricken, smitten of God, and afflicted. But He was wounded for our transgressions, He was bruised for our iniquities: the chastisement of our peace was upon Him; and with His stripes we are healed. All we like sheep have gone astray; we have

turned every one to his own way; and the LORD hath laid on Him the iniquity of us all. He was oppressed, and He was afflicted, yet He opened not His mouth: He is brought as a lamb to the slaughter, and as a sheep before her shearers is dumb, so He openeth not His mouth. He was taken from prison and from judgment: and who shall declare His generation? For He was cut off out of the land of the living: for the transgression of My people was He stricken. And He made His grave with the wicked, and with the rich in His death; because He had done no violence, neither was any deceit in His mouth. Yet it pleased the LORD to bruise Him; He hath put Him to grief: when thou shalt make His soul an offering for sin, He shall see His seed, He shall prolong His days, and the pleasure of the LORD shall prosper in His hand. He shall see of the travail of His soul, and shall be satisfied: by His knowledge shall My righteous servant justify many; for He shall bear their iniquities. Therefore will I divide Him a portion with the great, and He shall divide the spoil with the strong; because He hath poured out His soul unto death: and He was numbered with the transgressors; and He bare the sin of many, and made intercession for the transgressors."

I told her in just this scripture alone, I can point out eight prophecies that Jesus fulfilled, even though he came along almost seven hundred years later. She wanted to see how, so I carefully explained each one that I saw.

1. Isaiah says that the Messiah would be "rejected by many." While Jesus was on the cross, He was mocked, blasphemed, and reviled even by the ones who were crucified with Him.

2. Isaiah says that the Messiah would "bear our sins and suffer in our place." This is what Christians believe Jesus did on the cross. Through His wounds we have been healed.

3. Isaiah says that the Messiah would "heal many." All who believe in Jesus and what He did for us are healed!

4. Isaiah says that the Messiah "voluntarily took our punishment upon Himself." No one made Jesus do this; as a matter of fact, Jesus said that He was the "Good Shepard, and the Good Shepard lays down His life for His sheep."

5. Isaiah says that the Messiah would "remain silent during His suffering." Jesus did not defend himself to Pontius Pilate, Herod, or even the Sanhedrin before His brutal crucifixion.

At this point she stopped me and said that I did not have to say anymore prophecies. She said that she found them convincing and had never heard this before. I told her that I read of a study somewhere that someone did in the science of probability. It set out the odds of one man in all of history fulfilling only eight of the possible two hundred and seventy possible prophecies in the Old Testament fulfilled by the life in Christ. The probability of Jesus only fulfilling eight prophecies according to this calculation would be 1 in 1,017.

We had a great discussion. We talked about the moral law and how Jesus came to fulfill it. It was a great time. We exchanged phone numbers, and I even gave her my Bible in the hope that she would begin to read the New Testament for the first time. She even came to church with me for a few services. We lost touch over time, but a seed definitely was planted, and I do pray that she has come to know Jesus as her Messiah.

The comical part about the day was that my sister apologized to me for taking so long. I had been at this bar with this woman talking for over three hours! I told my sister it was a very awesome day and thanked her for wanting me to accompany her. I had made the best of the day, and more importantly, my sister was just fine after her appointment.

The Lord truly was working in my life. Wherever I went, I saw how good He truly is. It is amazing how the Holy Spirit can work through you all for God's glory when you are a Christian.

An excellent example of this was when I had seen my family physician and he had to call in a prescription. It was nothing life-threatening, just some medication I needed to take temporarily. Everything seemed to be normal until I went to pick it up. As I pulled in front of the pharmacy, I realized that I'd had the doctor call the prescription in to the wrong place!

I called the doctor back the following day, and the receptionist said that they did not know which pharmacy the prescription had been called into. The only thing they could give me was a phone number.

I thought to myself, *What is going on here? This should not be so complicated!*

I Googled the phone number and found that it was at a pharmacy very near my house. I was at work and had a church board meeting that night, so I figured that I would just pick it up after the meeting, thinking that most pharmacies were open twenty-four hours.

Long story short, I was wrong, and at 9:30 p.m. I drove there, and the store was closed. I was getting very frustrated over all of this.

The following morning I was to start new hours at my job, which would be 10:00 a.m. to 7:00 p.m. I had recently taken yet another pay cut and decided to voluntarily step down from my position as a supervisor and request a change of job functions. My request was granted, and I was excited to start a new role in the reprographics and copy center side of our department.

I got up that morning, took my daughter to her Christian daycare, and then headed over to the right pharmacy. I pulled into the parking lot, and it was open!

I walked into the store and back to the pharmacy section, where I found that the cage was down and the lights were off. I walked back to the front of the store and asked when the pharmacy opened. They said at nine o'clock.

I looked at my watch and noticed that it was 8:15 a.m. Forty-five minutes? I said, "Thank you" very nicely, smiled, and walked out of the store.

I said to God in a private conversation, "Either You do not want me to have this prescription for some reason, or I am just one foolish person! I am getting so frustrated because of my initial stupidity for having it called in to the wrong place and am getting what I deserve—Lord, I learned my lesson!"

I went home, studied a little bit, and waited until nine o'clock. I got back to the store at 9:07 a.m. and walked to the back. The lights were on in the pharmacy, and the cage was up!

There were two women with white coats on behind the counter, so I knew I was in business. I walked to the counter and a young woman yelled across from the back, "Can I help you?"

I said, "I hope so. If this store did not have my prescription, I am going to presume that the good Lord does not want me to have it! You have no idea what I have been through."

She chuckled and asked what my name was. She punched it up and said that nothing had been called in under my name.

I said, "Are you serious?"

She then asked for my doctor's name. She punched information up on her computer and found that nothing was called in for me by his office.

Fuming on the inside, I thanked her and was about to leave when the other woman asked me what the prescription was for.

I told her, and she said that they had a mystery prescription that was called in, had no idea who it was for or who it was called in by, and she had it. There must have been a glitch in the system somehow.

I said, "Praise God."

The younger woman called me over to get some information and then said that I could walk around the store or something because it would take about twenty minutes to process.

I looked around and the store was empty. What was I going to do for twenty minutes? Go up and down each aisle, read greeting cards, look at candy, medications, or cheap children's toys?

I then felt led to say to her, "Do you mind if I just stay here and talk to you while you process my information? I am married, so I am not trying to pick you up. Just trying to pass time."

She said that she didn't mind and would like that very much. She told me that she was having a very bad year and wanted to know a little more about my faith in God since she heard me say some things about Him, and that she was a Christian but had lost her faith.

I told her that I did not know the details of what was going on in her life, but I did know that Jesus loved her so much. I then asked her if she was familiar with the story in the Bible when Jesus called Peter out of the boat and he walked on water.

She said that she had heard it before, but it had been a long time, and that she had not been to church in quite some time either.

I said, "I'll sum it up for you quickly. Well, the disciples were inside of a boat while Jesus was on land, off to pray. Evening came and the boat drifted into the midst of the sea, and a windy storm came, which made the boat toss all around from the waves. They then looked out on the sea, and they thought they saw a spirit coming toward them walking on the water, and they were frightened. As it got closer, Jesus said it was He and not to be scared. Peter then said if it truly was Him then he should let Peter come onto the water. Do you know what happened next?"

She said, "Peter walked onto the water, right?"

I said, "Bingo! Jesus told him to come, and Peter had an experience that cannot be explained by science and transcended the laws of logic and nature. I mean, people don't just walk on water naturally, but when you have faith in Jesus, you can do anything! But what happened next in the story?"

She said, "I think Peter then fell in the water, right?"

I said, "Yes, he did, but more importantly, do you know why?"

She said, "Honestly, I really don't. I never really thought about it. I mean, Jesus was there, so why did he sink?"

I said, "It is because Peter saw the stormy wind and became afraid. Ya see, this happens to all of us. Because Peter took his eyes off of Jesus and focused on the high waves, the wind, and all that was around him, his faith wavered when he realized what he was doing."

She said, "Oh, I see. I kind of get it now. But what does this really have to do with me and my faith?"

I said, "It has to do with everything about you and your faith. Think about it. The reality of our Christian lives is that though we may not walk on water, we do walk through some difficult situations. If we focus on the waves or the wind of the difficult circumstances around us without looking to Jesus first for help, we too will be in despair and often sink. To maintain our faith when situations are difficult, we need to keep our eyes focused on Jesus's power rather than our inadequacies."

I took a good look at her, and she was beginning to tear up. I knew that I had hit something in her heart and mind that affected her and what she was going through. I put my hand on her shoulder and said, "This doesn't necessarily mean that you have failed. Look at what Peter did next!"

She said, "What did he do?" as she wiped her eye with a tissue.

I said, "When Peter began to sink, he said, 'Lord, save me!' Peter then reached out to Jesus, whose hand was already stretched out to catch him. Peter was afraid, but he still looked to Jesus. Jesus then saved him and said to him, 'Oh, Peter, ye of little faith, why did you doubt?" Then I asked, "Are you having issues with doubt?"

She nodded her head as she wiped another tear.

I said, "You see, when we are apprehensive about the troubles around us and doubt Christ's presence or ability to help, we must remember that He is the only one that can really help us. Our families, our friends, our coworkers, the world, or maybe even your church has let you down, but not Jesus. He never will. Focus on Him."

While we were talking, there was still no one in line behind me, but the drive-thru part of the pharmacy was getting very busy, and the other woman was frantically working. The young woman who I was talking to took notice, said that she lost track of time, and said that she had better get back to work.

The woman who was working, who was her supervisor, was overhearing our conversation, heard her say that, and yelled, "Don't you dare! I will take care of this. You need to hear what he is saying. He was sent here for a reason."

I said, "Yes, I was. I came here to pick up a prescription."

We all had a nice laugh.

The young woman I was speaking with was in tears and said that there was a reason why I came to that store that morning at that particular moment. She said that I was a messenger from God. Although I do not think I was a messenger of God, the bottom line is that she needed to hear what I had to say and that Jesus loves her. God restored her faith in Him through me that morning. We talked at that counter for about forty-five minutes. God is just so good! I was a blessing to her, and she blessed me as well.

People come in and out of our lives every day; it is up to all of us as Christians to share the love of God. This experience just showed me more of the meaning of 1 Corinthians 12:6: "And there are diversities of operations, but it is the same God which worketh all in all."

When you become a Christian, you become one of God's communication channels. We must be alert to all opportunities that God makes available to us. This means *all opportunities.*

I never in my wildest dreams would have thought that I would be witnessing to a Jewish woman at a bar or encouraging and building up in the faith a fellow Christian who had lost her faith at a pharmacy while I am picking up a prescription; but that is just it—I am not in control, God is.

God is omnipotent, which comes from "omni," meaning "all" and "potent" meaning "power." He has all power over all things, at all times, in all ways, and power over all the works of grace in the hearts of all Christians. This inward power comes from the Holy Spirit and makes Christians fit for wonderful things, so we need to be prepared at all times!

This woman needed some advice and counsel; she had given up going to church and lost faith to some degree. Where was she going to get it?

What I have come to learn is that if I have knowledge of the truth, or any power to make it known, godly advice or counsel, it all comes from the Holy Spirit living and working inside of me, and all the glory goes to God! It was not by chance I was there.

I left that pharmacy on a high like I had never had before in my life. I had walked into the store about an hour prior feeling pretty frustrated and questioning myself and God about why I had been running in circles to pick up this prescription in the first place. I now had my answer—it was not about me anymore, it was about this woman. God was showing me some really awesome things, how He works, and my understanding was that I really had a lot to learn! Just when you think you have it all figured out, you come to realize that you are far from knowing anything at all.

I even thought I was getting pretty well-rounded in my studies, but then I stumbled on a YouTube video that opened the door to a whole new branch of Christianity that I never knew about!

I remember it like it was yesterday, and I was definitely not prepared for it. I clicked on an icon that brought me to a video entitled, "Atheism vs. Christianity. Which way does the evidence point?" If you have ever seen a kid out front of a candy store waiting for the door to open with their eyes lit up, that was me!

It was moderated by a guy named Lee Strobel, who I had never heard of, who was the pastor of the church where this debate was being held. It was at Willow Creek Community Church in South Barrington, Illinois, recorded on June 27, 1993, so it was an old video. Although it was recorded when I was a junior in high school, I did not care; I was ready to hear each side, and more importantly, to do my best not to have bias for either side. The best part about it is that it was over two hours long! I wanted to be as neutral as I could be and let whichever argument persuade me as it could.

The news media was there, and it was being broadcasted live all over the radio. They wanted to have the best possible atheist debater and defender of Christianity in the world to present their case based on facts and evidence, staying away from emotionalism that clouds the issues from either side.

So they introduce the atheist who was going to argue for the side of atheism by the name of Frank Zindler. He was an outspoken atheist whose credentials were impeccable. He held a BS of biology from the University of Michigan, an MA in Geology from Indiana University, and was a PhD candidate at Suny Albany. He was an author, had been on radio talk shows, and was very active in the atheist community. He was in favor of the Christ myth hypothesis. They then said, "He is here to debunk the mythology, which is your Bible, and to demonstrate why atheism is the philosophy that makes sense. He was also going to explain why atheists believe your God is make-believe."

I said to myself, "Who could possibly compete with someone like that who is a Christian? I have debated many people, but not to this caliber. I would have been highly intimidated if I was the one who was about to debate him."

They then introduce this guy by the name of Dr. William Lane Craig, who is a Christian philosopher. He earned a doctorate in philosophy at the University of Birmingham in England and a second doctorate in theology at the University of Munich, in Germany. Then for two years he studied the historicity of the resurrection of Jesus.

My jaw dropped. I had no idea that there were studies like this in the world! These two gentlemen were highly educated, intelligent, and spent many years studying their subjects. I felt like such a pion! I was so ready to hear this debate!

Dr. Craig then defined the Christian theology that he was going to defend by saying that God exists and revealed Himself through Jesus Christ, and it was not the fine points of Christianity that Christians themselves differ on. He was going to defend two basic contentions. One is that there is no good evidence that atheism is true, and two that there is good evidence that Christianity is true.

So for over two hours I glued myself to my computer screen and sat at attention. I listened to each side present their arguments and remained neutral and let the arguments do their work. At the end, I must say that Dr. Craig truly destroyed Mr. Zindler's arguments from the starting gun to the finish line. He had him from his opening statement until his closing remarks. Mr. Zindler and the atheistic argument failed on all accounts.

I know that it is only a matter of personal opinion to think that Dr. Craig clearly won the debate, but apparently I was not the only person who thought this way.

There were a total of 7,778 in attendance for this debate.

6,168 people filled out surveys at the end.

Ninety-seven percent of the surveys voted that the case for Christianity was most compelling.

The unbelievable part was that 82 percent of the 632 non-Christians voted that the case for Christianity was stronger!

The best part about it was that forty-seven unbelievers who came to the event became Christians that night.

Not one Christian left as an atheist.

This was just incredible, and I had to learn more about apologetics because I had found a new passion.

I had come to learn that I was an amateur apologist from the beginning, even before I made a decision to become a Christian. I let the evidence and the moral argument lead me to Jesus. Just by engulfing myself with study about various world religions and philosophies, I was learning how to defend the Christian faith outside of the Bible. I now was able to sculpt the way I thought with better arguments by studying apologetics from men and women in the field who have dedicated their lives to defending the faith. There sure was a wealth of information out there, and I wanted to know about it all!

I began with William Lane Craig and his ministry, watched all of his debates, and then looked into the guy who moderated the first debate I watched, Lee Strobel, who was a pastor. His story of coming to Christ was just incredible because before he was a Christian, he was an atheist. Most of the apologists I had encountered were atheists or agnostics before they were Christians, and they let the compelling evidence lead them to the truth of the Christianity. Some were Christians struggling with doubt about the faith, and then by studying apologetics, their faith was strengthened by the arguments for Christianity.

I was introduced to other apologists, great ones like Norman Geiszler, Frank Turek, Kyle Butt, and countless others; but then there was Michael Licona, who I truly admired, and whose mentor was Gary Habermas, who I had a fond and mad respect for.

Gary had a debate in 1985 against Antony Flew, a well-known, intelligent, and scholarly atheist at the time, to argue whether or not the resurrection of Jesus was an actual historical and physical event, live in front of three thousand people. There were five philosophers there, and four of them judged that Gary had won while the other philosopher was undecided. There were also five judges, and three of them voted in favor of Gary.

Obviously the evidence that Gary presented was overwhelming to have most of the professionals vote in favor of his arguments. It is also rumored that before Antony Flew's death in April 2010, he now believed in the existence of God.

Could have this conversion have been a bit influenced by Gary's arguments?

I guess no one will ever truly know, but I do believe everyone should take the time to listen to the debate, make up their own minds, and see what the evidence leads them to believe is true.

It is no easy task to leave something that you have believed to be true your entire life. To give up one's worldview is probably one of the hardest things anyone can ever do in life, but what we must do is ask ourselves: Would we rather live a lie than live for the truth?

It is a very humbling experience; I mean, I did it, so I understand. Swallowing your pride and admitting that you were wrong goes against human nature. It takes the power of God and His enlightenment to show us our errors. Though we may be able to persuade the mind, it is up to God to change the heart.

There are many fine apologists out there, but I began learning from church history about the original apologists who came on to the scene and battled early heresies that were creeping into the church. It was awesome to see these fine men protect the word of God.

I was really enlightened and was learning so much about the power of persuasion. We need to have a good defense for what we believe, have a good understanding what others believe, and do what we can to destroy arguments and false philosophies and bring people to the knowledge of the truth about the Christian faith.

Beware lest any man spoil you through philosophy and vain deceit, after the tradition of men, after the rudiments of the world, and not after Christ. (Colossians 2:8)

Paul used apologetics all throughout the book of Acts, and here is one example: "And he reasoned in the synagogue every sabbath, and persuaded the Jews and the Greeks" (Acts 18:4).

The New Testament also records and instructs us that we as Christians should be able to defend our faith:

But sanctify the Lord God in your hearts: and be ready always to give an answer to every man that asketh you a reason of the hope that is in you with meekness and fear. (1 Peter 3:15)

Casting down imaginations, and every high thing that exalteth itself against the knowledge of God, and bringing into captivity every thought to the obedience of Christ. (2 Corinthians 10:5)

Holding fast the faithful word as he hath been taught, that he may be able by sound doctrine both to exhort and to convince the gainsayers. (Titus 1:9)

I have encountered some Christians who if asked a tough question by an unbeliever and did not know how to answer it, would just say, "You just have to believe by faith."

The above scriptures clearly tell us we need to give reasons, always be ready to give answers, cast down imaginations, exhort and convince, and so on.

The bottom line is we need to defend what we believe and live for what we know as true.

CHAPTER 8

Conversions

Being a dad was such a tremendous responsibility but such an awesome blessing at the same time. My daughter was such a joy to be around, and to think I had another child on the way was very scary but wonderful. It would be nice to see our daughter have a brother or sister to play and grow up with.

One beautiful, hot summer day, I decided to take my three-year-old daughter to the park near our house. We were walking on a trail that wrapped around a very small lake. At the time, we had her enrolled in a really nice Christian daycare, and how she loved to talk and hear about Jesus! She had such childlike faith and asked the most inquisitive questions! This really made me happy, and I could only hope that someday she would become a Christian.

As we were walking, taking in the beautiful scenery, watching people ride their bikes, walking, and sweating from the extremely hot sun, she looked up at me with her baby blue-greenish eyes and said, "Daddy, what is heaven like?"

I was a bit taken aback by her question and did not know what to say. It really caught me off-guard as we had just recently been talking about something entirely off the subject.

I wanted to make sure that as a Christian dad, I answered her questions to the best of my ability. I did not want her to grow up misguided about the Christian faith like so many other children who thought that angels looked like a little baby wearing diapers with cute white wings, playing a harp, and looking like cupid sitting on clouds in heaven. I wanted her faith to be directly from biblical teachings and Cupid certainly was not.

I thought about what 1 Corinthians 2: 9–10 said:

> But as it is written, Eye hath not seen, nor ear heard, neither have entered into the heart of man, the things which God hath prepared for them that love Him. But God hath revealed them unto us by his Spirit: for the Spirit searcheth all things, yea, the deep things of God.

I knew that she would certainly not be able to grasp any concept of what heaven was like from that scripture, but after some quick thinking, I decided to go with my gut and draw an analogy from this scripture that a three-year-old may be able to understand.

I said, "Sweetie, this is a great question! Now what I want you to do is take a moment and answer the following questions. I'll say them one by one, okay?"

She said, "Okay, Daddy."

I said, "What is your favorite thing to smell?"

She said, "Hmmmn, I think that would be puppy breath!"

I said, "Oh, just like your mommy! Okay, now what is your favorite thing to touch? You know, like something that feels nice."

She said, "A puppy's hair because it feels so soft!"

I said, "Good one! They sure are soft! Okay, now what is your favorite thing to taste?

She said, "That's easy! Chocolate ice cream!"

I said, "Oh boy! That sure is yummy in your tummy! Now what is your favorite thing to look at?"

She said, "I guess princesses with their pretty dresses and tiaras!"

I said, "I think I knew you were going to say that! Okay, this is the last question. Now this may sound funny, but what is your favorite noise to hear?"

She said, "I guess really pretty music!"

I said, "That is great. Now I want you to stop and just close your eyes for a minute and no peeking! I want you to imagine a place where all of these things are going on at the same time and going on forever. Now what would you think of a place like that?"

She said, "Wow! That would be great, Daddy! Is that what heaven is going to be like?"

I said, "Nope. Heaven will be nothing like that."

She looked at me with a very confused look on her face, and she said, "Huh?"

I patted her on her head and said, "Heaven will be much better."

You see, I really have no idea what heaven was actually going to be like. I can draw some contexts and parallels from the book of Revelation, but at the same time there are so many different ways to interpret them. I wanted to be as honest as I could with her, and I think I did just that. I left it in the hands of her five senses and imagination, knowing in all honestly that it truly was beyond our understanding.

She was such an amazing little girl. I remember one summer we had just gotten home from a family vacation. We spent a week at the beach. After everyone was in bed, as well as me, and I just laid there thinking about how much of a blessing it was to get away for a week.

I was thinking about how many times in life we can allow the purpose that God has for each and every one of us to be buried deep within us because of our daily routines. It is easy to let the busyness of life to get in the way of our walk with Christ. Making money, paying the bills, and often fulfilling all of life's demands can leave little time to explore our inner desires and our purpose as Christians.

Unless you are active in a part-time or full-time ministry, attending regular Bible studies, reading your Bible daily, the secular world's influence can be very damaging to your spiritual health.

I felt so bad for the many people in the world who had been swept along by the waves of life. I hoped and prayed that they may be able to find the time to take a break and discover the wonderful works of God once again just as we were able to do as a family the week prior on vacation.

I was just lying there praising and thanking God for the time I was able to take away from the busyness of life. We as a family were able to meditate together on God's wonderful works of His awesome creation. As I had always done, I did my best to understand God's precepts by reading the word of God on vacation, applying what I learned to my life, and making an impact on others because there is never a vacation from that!

I was dwelling on the fact that people who live by the ocean may take for granted the wonderful works of God. As I had time to walk along the beach with my daughter and observe the mighty ocean's waves, my three-year-old once again was filled with many fascinating questions.

She wanted to know everything from how many pebbles were in the sand to what kind of fish were in the water to how many stars were in the black infinite space overhead. I answered each and every question by telling her that they are the wonderful works of God and going into detail to the best of my ability to explain the love God has for His creation, especially human beings.

I thanked the good Lord for the memories that were made that week, and I was also thankful for the time my family and I were able to meditate on His wonderful works.

I understood that there were many people who were not able to get away for a week, but if I could just have a moment with them and give a bit of advice, I would say to spend some time being still each day. Instead of leaping out of bed and rushing out the door, set their alarm clocks a little earlier to allow some time to meditate on God's word, or take a walk and observe God's creation because it is all around them.

I would tell them to pause and listen to the still, small voice of the Holy Spirit speaking to them through His wonderful works as the good word says in Psalm 119:27: "Make me understand the way of Your precepts; so shall I meditate on Your wonderful works."

I knew that I could never make my daughter be a Christian, but I could allow the Holy Spirit to guide me to give the answers she needs through His marvelous creation and pray that someday she makes a decision to follow Christ.

She was such a sweet little girl, and believe it or not, I really learned a lot from her. She just melted my heart every day, but that particular Halloween, she really made me lose it with joyful tears.

We had just gotten back from trick or treating, and she had tons of tasty candy. The problem was that we had been murdered with trick or treaters that came to our door, and we had given out all of our candy.

All of a sudden there was a knock at the door.

My daughter went to go answer it because she wanted to give out some candy to the trick or treaters.

I told her not to answer the door because we were out of candy. I just had forgotten to turn out the outside porch light. I also said as soon as they went away, I would shut it off.

This is when she just melted my heart.

She said, "Daddy, don't turn the light off. I have plenty of candy; I'll just share."

So for the remainder of the night, I watched as my daughter answered the door and gave away the candy that she worked so hard for.

I looked at my wife and said, "We must be doing something right."

All of the wonderful things I was observing, learning, and beginning to understand I was also sharing with my family and close friends. It turns out that the seeds that I was planting began to take root and be watered by God, and this was evident in my good friend, my boss at work.

He was raised in a Roman Catholic home and even went to Roman Catholic school through his elementary and high school years. He admitted though that he was never a believer. He then had a series of events unfold in his life that could not be explained by a natural understanding, only supernatural, and he gave his life to Christ. He began going to church with me and was baptized by my pastor, and it was a glorious day. He had a new outlook on life and was so hungry to grow in the faith.

Then, a short time later, through a friend of mine, I met someone, and she found out I was a chaplain. This young woman contacted me and asked if she could talk to me in person.

Of course, I happily obliged. It turned out that she had a pretty miserable year and really needed to talk to someone. Something had happened that had torn her up and changed her completely. She had been trying to deal with it on her own, but she could not move on. It had been a year, and she thought she would naturally move on from it, but she couldn't, and every day she had a constant feeling of guilt.

She was living in the "what if" world and could not move on. She needed some type of closure and did not know where to turn. She said that she felt that she had a connection with God, really wanted to change, but was unsure how to do it.

She was feeling miserable, uncomfortable, terrified, brokenhearted, and tried to deal with all of this on her own but just could not do it anymore. She then finally asked if I could help her.

I sat patiently and listened to her pour her heart out.

I finally said, "What I can help you with is three aspects of forgiveness that do not come by natural means, only by the supernatural. They are forgiving yourself, which is hard; forgiving the people who hurt you, which is harder; and attaining the best forgiveness of all, from God, which is the easiest because the debt has already been paid. It really is not me that is going to help; I am going to point you to Jesus. He is the one and only person that can heal you if you are willing."

Her eyes lit up, and she wanted to know more. We talked for a couple of hours, and there were a lot of tears. In the course of events that unfolded in our conversation, she asked Jesus to be her Lord and Savior and therefore attained the forgiveness that she truly needed.

I gave her a Bible and told her to begin reading it from the book of John. I also told her that the Bible was based on promises, not feelings, and once she began to believe the promises, the feelings would come.

From that moment on she was a new creation in Christ. She and even her friends began to come to church with me, Bible study, and were baptized by my pastor. As you can see, my pastor and I became a great team! This woman became such an awesome ambassador for Christ and is now, I am proud to say, leading many others to Jesus.

About a month later, I heard that a friend of mine from high school who I had not seen in many years was about to become a Mormon and was being baptized into the Church of Latter-day Saints.

I just felt that I was led to contact him immediately.

I got in touch with him and told him that I was concerned. I told him that I was a Christian now, I had studied Mormon theology, and it was one of the strangest theologies that I had ever learned about.

I asked him if he understood what he was doing.

He said that he was not really sure, but an elder of the church had been taking him to church. We had a long conversation, and instead of discrediting Mormon theology and Joseph Smith (the founder of Mormonism), I figured I would just go right to the vast claims in the Book of Mormon that have been debunked by the secular world. It describes an ancient civilization with cities, temples, animals, swords, shields, and countless other artifacts, but the major problem was that there had been no archeological finds confirming this.

I explained to him how archeology plays such a significant role in evidence. When a historical claim is made in history, artifacts that are found will usually back up the claim. The Bible had countless artifacts and sites with worthy excavation to support many of its claims in both the Old and New Testaments.

The Book of Mormon had none, zero, zilch.

I asked him if he was really familiar with the Book of Mormon.

He said that he had been given a copy, but he had not read it. I told him that when he had a chance to open it and read Mormon 6:10–15, which describes a bloody battle scene at the Hill Cumorah in New York, southeast of Rochester. According to the Book of Mormon, hundreds of thousands of people were killed on or near there, and it even goes so far to say that they were not buried.

Compare this to to the Battle of Gettysburg, where it is estimated that roughly six thousand soldiers were killed and four thousand were wounded.

I told him that this is where the problem arises. Bullets by the thousands and all types of other artifacts were found at Gettysburg, so wouldn't he think that at least something would have been found at this hill in New York?

People have investigated this area and not found a single piece of evidence that this great battle took place. With the sheer number of people that died, artifacts, weapons, and even armor would simply have to be found.

I even went so far to tell him a paper was written by a man named Professor Thomas Stuart Ferguson in 1975. He dedicated twenty-five years of his life solely to archeological digs to discover proof supporting the Book of Mormon. After twenty-five years, nothing was found in the geography of the Book of Mormon, and he called it fictional. Still to this day, nothing has ever been found.

We had a very fruitful discussion, and he asked me to come over to visit him. He said that I had changed a lot since high school, and he remembered me as the small, tough kid who could handle my hands well in a fight.

We had some laughs, and I told him about my conversion. He said that he had given his heart to Jesus a couple of times, but it had no effect.

I said to him that God didn't work that way, and if he sincerely believed that he had given God his heart, then he had. I had my Bible and turned to Romans 10:9 and read it to him out loud: "That if thou shalt confess with thy mouth the Lord Jesus, and shalt believe in thine heart that God hath raised him from the dead, thou shalt be saved."

I asked him if he had done this. Did he truly believe it in his heart?

He said that he did not, and I told him that this was why he had not truly given his heart to Jesus. So right then and there, I asked him if he wanted to, and he then accepted Jesus Christ as his Lord and Savior. He had goose bumps when he was done.

Now this gentleman lived about forty-five minutes away from me, so plugging him into my church was out of the question, but I did help him find a church in his area, and we stay in touch off and on. I am happy to report that he loves being a Christian, and it has changed his life significantly.

The elders from the Mormon Church gave up on him, and I told him if they tried contacting him again, I would be more than willing to talk with them anytime.

A short time thereafter, we had a young man at our church who was going through some issues. We became good friends, and I knew his mother and father very well. He was not a Christian, but he did go to church sometimes.

I was twice his age, but I could relate to the challenges, the temptations, and the general life of being a young man. He met a young woman online and decided to move in with her, and she lived three hours away. Obviously his family, friends, and I were very concerned about his decision.

He was old enough to make his own decisions, good or bad, and he reminded me so much of myself. People like us often need to learn things the hard way. His mind was made up, so he packed his things and the young woman and her mother came to pick him up one evening.

Before he left, I told him that I really thought he was making a bad decision, but he was a grown man and was responsible for his actions. However, I also threw out a lifeline for him. I told him that if at any point down the road he felt that he had made the wrong decision, I would pick him up and take him home with no judgement and no questions asked. I said that all he had to do was let me know he was ready to come home. He thanked me but said that he would be fine.

The next morning he was gone. His friends and family were really upset about it, especially his mother. Life went on the best it could without him. We prayed for him daily, and then about a month later, our prayers seem to have been answered when I received a text message from him reading, "I am ready to come home."

I responded by asking for the address where he was located. Once I had it, I told him I would see him the next morning.

The next morning I filled my gas tank up and took the three-hour drive to pick him up. He was outside waiting with all of his belongings. He threw his things in my trunk, and we were off for the three-hour ride back the way I came.

I did not say a word. I figured I would wait until he decided to start a conversation, and then he just began to cry. I just put my arm around him, and when he was done crying he began to confide in me.

He told me many things. He was damaged, brokenhearted, had been abused his entire twenty-one years, and felt as if every decision he made in his life was wrong.

I just felt led to tell him the story of the prodigal son.

I asked him if he had ever heard the story before, and he said that he had not. I then asked him to grab my Bible that was lying on the back seat, turn to Luke 15:11–32, and read it out loud.

When he was finished reading, I said, "What did you think of that story? Did it remind you of anyone you know?"

He said, "Yeah. A little bit, except for the ending. I really think I am lost."

I said, "We are all lost without God. But the good news is that He loves us so much that He seeks all of us out and rejoices when we are found. Jesus, throughout the Gospels, associates with sinners because He wants to bring home the lost, or people who seem to be beyond hope or hopeless. Even before I was a believer, God was seeking me out, and you can trust that He is seeking you out, buddy."

He said, "Well, I do feel hopeless and like a complete failure."

I said, "God loves you anyway, brother. I was like you once—immature, rebellious, and wanted to live life the way I wanted. We are very similar to the story you just read. We hit rock bottom before we finally come to our senses. This is why you remind me so much of myself."

He said, "What do you mean, man? You are a chaplain! I'm sure you never did anything wrong in your life."

I just laughed for a little bit, because I remembered that he did not know my whole story, and finally I said, "Bud, if you only knew how much I value God's grace. I have probably doubled or even tripled the number of things you regret doing in your life."

He said, "Really?"

I said, "Yeah, man. Trust me. It often takes much sorrow for people to finally look to the only one who can help. Like the old me, you are trying to live life your own way, and by doing this you have selfishly pushed aside any responsibility that gets in your way. I know for a fact that I hurt many people when I lived like this, and I only wish I could have saved myself and family the grief I caused them by the life that I led. The worst part is that I hurt God in the process."

He said, "Yeah, tell me about it."

I said, "But we cannot turn back the hands on the clock, we can only move forward, and like the ending of the story you read, though we messed up, when the prodigal son returned home, where was his father?"

He said, "Waiting for him?"

I said, "Yes, but even more than that! His father watched and patiently waited for him. He understood he was dealing with someone with a rebellious heart and a will of his own, but he was ready to greet him when and if he returned. When he finally did, what an amazing moment for the both of them! In the same way, my young friend, God's love for us is very patient and welcoming. He searches and gives us opportunities to respond, but He will never force us to come to Him. Like the father in the story, He waits patiently for us to come to our senses. Does that make sense?"

He said, "Yeah, it does. Do you think my mom and dad are going to be mad at me?"

I said, "No, I think they will be very happy, but you do have a long road ahead of you."

We talked for most of the ride, and when I finally dropped him off, his parents were so happy to see him. It was a great day.

The following day was Sunday, and he came to church with his parents. I talked with him briefly before the service, and after the service I went home.

He then called me on the phone and asked me to come over as soon as I could. I had a really good feeling about this call. I grabbed my Bible and an extra one that was a Life Application Study Bible.

His dad was out, but his mother was upstairs taking a nap. He said that he thought about our conversation in the car a lot, and after the sermon today, he felt that it was time to become a Christian. I asked him if he knew what he was doing, and he said that he did and that he was more than ready. He said that he wanted to wake his mom up so she could be there because she would be very happy.

Then and there, my young friend asked Jesus to be his Lord and Savior. He said that it was the first time in his life he actually felt at peace. I gave him the Life Application Study Bible and told him to keep it and begin reading it from the book of John as soon as possible. He and his mother had very joyful tears streaming down their faces, and I left the house as they embraced each other. His mother just looked up at me and said, "Thank you."

I pointed up and said, "No thanks necessary, and don't thank me, thank God."

I gave her a friendly wink and walked out the front door.

Since becoming a Christian, I don't think there is anything that gives me more joy being a part of guiding someone else to becoming a Christian. It is an indescribable feeling, but if I had to choose one word, I would say "awesome."

I pictured in my mind when the young man's father came home and he told him what he had done. It brought a great big smile to my face imagining his father embracing him, like the story of the prodigal son, with tears in his eyes, saying something like, "You were lost, and now you are found."

He would no longer just have a son, but a brother in Christ. I could only hope for a miracle with my dad and the same thing happening for him and me. My father, my fellow brother in Christ? Who would ever believe that would happen?

CHAPTER 9

Change

I was really beginning to enjoy my new job description and my hours at my secular job. There was no traffic both on the way to and from work. The new tasks were challenging, and I was like a fish out of water, but it was a lot of fun to see how books were made from start to finish.

We would get a file from the client with a request for how many books they wanted. The file was often not perfect, and we would have to make changes to make sure that the pages would fall correctly. When you print a book, you don't want a page that was supposed to be on the front to be on the back or vice versa, so looking at a three hundred-page document took some time to make sure the book fell in order just right.

We had machines that could print books rather quickly. Whether it was in color or black and white, with or without tabs, single- or double-sided, we could print out 150 books with over one hundred pages in about four hours. We then would have to punch, bind, and close them.

This was a whole new world for me, and it was a very detailed process, but it got me thinking about how the Bible was put together and what the process was like many, many years ago.

The scribes in the early days did not have the luxury of going to a copy machine, pressing a button, entering how many copies they wanted, and then seeing the words magically appear on High-grade 8½-by-11-inch laser paper.

The earliest biblical texts were not printed; they were written by hand on scrolls made from a plant-based paper called papyrus or animal skin that was stitched together called parchment.

Maybe in the second or third century, the papyrus or parchment was folded and stitched into codex that resembled a modern book. Because being literate was not as common as it is nowadays, scribes were considered very special, and they were also considered editors.

The papyrus or parchment would be copied over and over again. It was a very meticulous and painstaking process, and sometimes minor mistakes occurred—insignificant errors such as incorrect punctuation or a missing letter, nothing detrimental that could change the message of any book or letter from the Bible. This entire process is known now as the transmission of the text.

This by no means makes the Bible filled with errors or mistakes. Scholars have looked back at the earliest copies, of which there are hundreds of thousands of early manuscripts, so we know that Bible we have today is very accurate and close to perfect since it began the transmission process.

It drives me crazy when people say that the church has altered the text throughout the years and therefore the Bible cannot be trusted. This is certainly not true. If someone does say that, the burden of proof is on him or her, so ask the person to give you examples.

It just gives me a deeper respect for how the Bible was put together over the years. It also makes me think how it makes my job so much easier when a client calls and orders 150 books.

I check the book on the computer to make sure it looks okay, send the amount requested to the copier machine, and presto—150 books are on their way! I do not have to copy by hand, letter by letter, word for word! It would take months, maybe even years to copy by hand 150 books and now technology has made it possible to get the job done in a matter of hours.

This is something early scribes would have given anything for!

Every time I pick up the Bible, I have the utmost respect for every word that I read after looking into the painstaking process of how the Bible was originally put together. I sit back in awe and wonder when I think about how the accuracy has been maintained since the beginning.

I was being trained by three different people who each had their own different style. Each one was right in the way that they did it, but I needed to find what fit best for me.

One gentleman who was training me was all in all an okay guy, had been in the business for a very long time, but was not very friendly, did not have good customer service skills, and was known to not have patience. He was the type of guy that if he taught you something once, you only had the chance to ask him the same question two more times after that, and if you needed to know again, you were on your own.

He was known to be very hard to get along with, but I just knew that I could affect this guy in a positive way—after all, I am a Christian.

We got friendly with each other, and he talked about his wife and son a lot. He liked basketball, and this is what limited his conversations, because he really did not have any other interests. He did not take care of himself healthwise. He was extremely overweight and did not exercise at all. He really did not do much to help the situation because he did not eat anything healthy. His diet consisted of meat, hotdogs, and sushi on Thursdays. I would never see vegetables or fruit on his plate for lunch. Breakfast always consisted of eggs and extra bacon. I guess you can see where I am going with this, and you can get a general idea of what kind of guy he is.

Anyhow, he was very ignorant, and I could tell that he was miserable. I really felt bad for him, and I just wished I could share Jesus with him at work. Then one day I got the opportunity because he started the conversation when no one else was around.

He said, "Ya know, Bill. I have to say that you are doing a great job. You really are picking up things rather quickly."

I said, "Thanks, man. I appreciate it. I guess you can take part of the reason for that; maybe it's because you are such a good teacher and have the patience of Job."

I was being sarcastic in a playful kind of way. He did know that, because he knew that he was not a good teacher and did not have any patience.

He laughed a little, and then said, "Yeah, I doubt that. Anyway, I'm curious man. I know that you have taken three pay cuts since you have been here. You have a wife, a kid, and another one on the way. What I don't get is that you always seem so happy. You have to tell me, how do you do it? I would never be able to do that! What is your secret?"

I wanted to be really careful on how I answered this, I didn't want to come off too religious, especially in a work setting.

I said, "Ya know, man, it really is not being happy. I am not happy at all about losing money, but I have constant joy in my heart that no one can ever take away. Life is not easy, and I know that, but it is my faith that gets me through."

He said, "Faith? How can faith do that?"

I said, "Because my focus is not on the here and now. I know that in this life there will be trials, tribulations, and hard times. If anyone says differently, then his or her faith will falter when times get hard. I know that my faith will get me through the good times and the bad times. The secret is to be content under any circumstance."

He said, "Wow. Under any circumstance? Sounds pretty difficult."

I said, "Well, it sure isn't easy, man, but that is where faith and hope come in."

At this point a couple of other employees walked through the door.

I said, "If you want to talk about it more, let me know; we can go to lunch away from here. This faith is available to you too. I would love to talk about it with you more someday soon, just let me know when. It will certainly change your life."

He said, "Sounds good."

I was very hopeful that he would say to me, "Let's go to lunch," one day soon, but life went on, and he was very miserable each and every day. His health got worse from not eating right and not exercising, and I was not the only person who noticed the slow decrease in his physical health and negative mood swings, but it was something that we all just dealt with.

I then was asked to do my first funeral, although just part of it, and it was quite an honor to be asked. A woman who I worked with was taking care of her mother. She ended up getting sick, and I made frequent visits to pray for her, but then the Lord saw fit to take her home.

Our pastor did most of the funeral service, but then I did about twenty minutes. I really enjoyed it a lot, I got my feet wet doing the funeral service process, and I really enjoyed it, even more so than doing weddings. I started to do funeral services more and more independently along with weddings.

Around this time my son was born, and I slowed down on doing services so I could spend more time at home. It was such a blessing to have a daughter and a son, and my wife and I decided that would be it for kids—we had one of each, and we were happy.

Not too long thereafter, my step-grandmother Gummy died. I ended up doing her funeral service, and now my dad had full access to his father's investments. He and his girlfriend decided to go their separate ways after over twenty years of being together. They put their house up for sale, and when it sold, she moved back to Long Island, New York, and my dad decided to move into an apartment about five miles from where he had lived.

My sisters and their other halves helped him move from one location to the other. We called our moving service "Hamburger Movers." It was an inside joke, and we got a lot of laughs from it. In this apartment, we all watched together as the New York Giants shocked the world by beating the undefeated New England Patriots. It was a great time for us. We had now watched a total of four Super Bowl wins by the New York Giants, and that would be the last time we watched the Giants win a Super Bowl together with my dad.

I had my concerns about him living by himself, but he was a grown man and was going to do what he wanted to do anyway. He also now had some money to play with and as he said, he could enjoy life now.

We had a conversation when he acquired this money, and it looked to me like in his mind the money was going to solve everything and be the secret to the happiness that he has been longing for. He could finally go on trips, gamble, and live as he pleased, but I told him that it would not fill the void in his heart.

He said, "What do you mean by that?"

I said, "There was a Christian philosopher from the sixteen hundreds by the name of Blaine Pascal. I was in the middle of reading some of his works. I would like to read you something, can I?"

He said, "As long as it is not too long."

I grabbed my Bible and I turned to John 7:38 because that is where I jotted down a note in the margin from Pascal.

I said, "What I am going to read to you is by Blaise Pascal from his volume entitled *Pensées* VII (425) 'What else does this craving, and this helplessness, proclaim but that there was once in man a true happiness, of which all that now remains is the empty print and trace? This he tries in vain to fill with everything around him, seeking in things that are not there the help he cannot find in those that are, though none can help, since this infinite abyss can be filled only with an infinite and immutable object; in other words by God himself.'"

I then said, "What do you think of that, Dad?"

He said, "I don't know what to think. I told you that I didn't want it to be too long, and I think it was."

I said, "I just want you to think about it. Christians have derived a quote from what Pascal said. They say, 'There is a God shaped vacuum in the heart of every man which cannot be filled by any created thing, but only by God, the Creator, made known through Jesus.' My fear, Dad, is that this is what you are going to try and do. You have been doing it your entire life. Sure, you have money now, you are going to buy things, try to fill this void, but you are truly not going to be at peace and have a purpose without God."

He said, "What do you mean? I should not spend my money and enjoy it?"

I said, "No. I do think you should enjoy yourself, but at the same time, if all you are going to do is try to fill this vacuum inside of your heart with things, you will never be at peace. I wrote that quote next to John 7:38, which says, "He that believeth on me, as the scripture hath said, out of his belly shall flow rivers of living water.""

He said, "Out of his belly?"

175

I said, "Ahh, you were listening. Yes, this was Jesus talking. The word *belly* is translated from Greek and means the "innermost being." Jesus was describing a spiritual empty place, not the physical stomach, for which the only solution is Jesus."

He said, "I told you church is for old people. If you were in charge of this money, you would probably give it all to the cult you belong to."

I said, "Dad, I am half your age, and I go to church, and I don't belong to a cult."

He said, "You belong to that cult!"

I said, "Cult? What do you mean by cult?"

He said, "You and all those other cult people."

I said, "Why is it a cult? Why would you say that? Do you even know what a cult is?"

He said, "It really doesn't matter. I think I am getting a dog and a new car."

I said, "Sounds like a plan. I think a dog would be good for you. You will have some responsibility; you will have to walk him, you know."

The conversation was getting off track, so I decided to just lay that one at rest. I do believe that it got him thinking though. All I wanted to do was plant a seed so that every time he spent some money, he would think, *Is this really filling my void?* I do believe I did just that.

He ended up adopting a four-year-old black Labrador retriever from a pet rescue. The dog had just recently been transported there from North Carolina. The dog, which he named Ralph, was a bait dog for pit bulls in illegal dog fighting. This dog was such a sweetheart, and my dad loved him very much and took him everywhere with him.

I was so busy with my ministry, home life, and work that I felt I was not as committed to Wesleyan theology as I had been when I first became a Christian. John Wesley played such an important role in my life, sculpted me into a wonderful way of thinking as a Christian, and he had done so much for Christianity. I did agree with much of Wesleyan thought, but there were some areas that I just did not wholeheartedly agree with anymore, and being a nondenominational chaplain, it made things a little more difficult for me to be a Wesleyan and a board member. I just could not find peace. I felt like a hypocrite, and I did not think it was fair to me or to the members of the church to have a board member who was not 100 percent committed to their theology. So after speaking with my pastor, I wrote the board members and the congregation a nice letter of withdrawal. I was still going to worship with them and go to Bible study, but as far as decision-making for the church, they needed to have someone who could adhere to all of the Wesleyan doctrine.

As time went on, my dad began to travel a little bit, and he even took Ralph when he could. He kept himself busy the best he could without having any interests, but he still slept a lot, and he seemed bored most of the time.

He told me that he wanted to move out of the apartment and buy a condominium in the development where he had lived with his girlfriend for many years. He bought one, and after renting a U-Haul truck for the day, the Hamburger Movers were gainfully employed once again.

It was a nice place, perfect for him, and great for Ralph, but he still had to walk him because his backyard consisted of some flower beds and a deck. He also hired a cleaning person that he became very friendly with.

His next mission for trying to fill this void I was talking about earlier was to get a fish tank. Not just a thirty-gallon tank, but one that was seventy to one hundred gallons and was very high maintenance. He understood how much work it was to keep it clean, and he knew that he did not want any part of it, but he would find a way to have it done.

He did this by becoming friendly with the fish guy who sold him the tank and the fish. He ended up hiring him and paying him under the table by the hour to take care of it. I'll tell ya, my dad was a piece of work. He was the only guy I knew who could do things like this. He and the fish guy became great friends and even drinking buddies. The guy was a little younger than me, and he looked at my dad kind of like a father figure.

The gentleman that trained me at work was now getting worse by the day. He was calling out sick a lot, had all kinds of doctors' appointments, and his physical features were getting really bad. I just felt that it was time to have a heart-to-heart with him, but the day I decided to do this he called out sick again. So what I did was write him a letter. I figured that I could leave it on his computer keyboard, and he could open it when he came into work that Monday.

I wrote:

> I am writing this letter to you because I am concerned about you. I asked our boss where you were this morning (Wednesday 12/17/14), and he said that you were out today for doctor appointments.

> My thoughts and prayers go out to you at this time, and my heart breaks for your physical condition, which is leading to an emotional and spiritual depression for you I am sure.

> We have been working together now for about two years, and I not only value you as a coworker, but I would like to consider you a friend.

> You once pulled me aside when we first started working together because you knew about my financial situation, how I kept getting mandatory pay cuts, and you did not understand how you could see me day in and day out be so happy and always having a smile on my face.

> Do you remember this conversation so far?

Anyhow, I told you it was because I was a Christian, I had a relationship with Jesus, I have learned to be content in any situation that life throws at me, and I learned to do as the Bible instructs to consider it pure joy.

In James 1:2 (Trials and Temptations) **it says,** "Consider it pure joy, my brothers and sisters, whenever you face trials of many kinds."

I then ended the conversation because we were in the workplace and I respect the fact that discussing religion is frowned on. But I ended the conversation with an invitation.

I said if you would like to know more, we could go to lunch some time, and that I would even buy.

That day I do believe in my heart that you learned something from me that you did not understand before. You saw the difference between people who say they are Christians and someone actually being a Christian. Now don't get me wrong, I am by no means perfect in any way, shape, or form, but the fact of the matter is that is the whole reason why I became a Christian.

I extended the invitation that day to you, but I never brought it up again in hope that you would consider talking about it more, but unfortunately, I never heard back from you.

Anyhow, I am writing to you now because I just care about you deeply, the entire staff here does, maybe some more than others, but we all do in our own way.

In my time working here I have seen two people pass away; one was a long process and one was unexpected that you saw with your own eyes.

It is heartbreaking to see people pass away that you work with, because if you think about it, coworkers actually spend more time with each other than their own families. We know so much about each other without even knowing each other too well just by spending so much time together.

This is exactly the point I am making with this, my friend. In the past two years that I have known you I have watched your health decline. You know it as well as all of us here, and now there are serious issues going on.

This is something that just cannot be ignored, and you must take action, get motivated, and do something about it. This is not only for you, but for your family.

Do you remember how hard your son took it when he learned of the passing of his teacher in that tragic car accident? I do believe you told me he was seeking some type of counsel for it.

Now could you imagine the pain he would go through if he lost his father at such an early age? The affects would be devastating.

I am not trying to make you feel bad, I am just trying to make you see that I care and that there are people who love and care about you very much, so consider this a form of tough love.

I have helped people with depression, had friends with it, and have also dealt with it myself—please forgive me if I am wrong, but I see the signs of depression in you.

You may feel that life sometimes may be pointless, or you have no capacity to handle what used to be the daily things of life, that no one understands or cares, that all is dark. You may imagine that you are in a swamp of quicksand unable to move. Nothing may be pleasurable anymore. I certainly do not know, only you do, my friend.

All I can do is remind you that you are worth something and that your life is extremely valuable. You have a family that loves you, people who care about you and want to see you get better, and most of all, and it may sound foolish, but God loves you.

They say that the mind appears to be where the physical and spiritual aspects of our beings connect. Undeniably, the wiring of our physical bodies can impact our souls. How exactly our bodies, souls,

and spirits function together in terms of our moods and emotions the Bible is not entirely clear. But God has not left us without weapons, nor has He abandoned us to struggle alone.

What I am supposed to do as a Christian is be filled with joy. Joy is something the Holy Spirit produces in the life of a follower of Jesus Christ. Joy is not about happiness. I am intentional about gratitude and focus on uplifting things even though many things may not be so uplifting.

I will say no more about this letter. Please when you are done reading it, just shred it. Take it for what it is worth; please get motivated to help yourself. God helps those who want to help themselves. God will help you, but only if you want to be helped.

God bless you, and I wish you and your family a very merry Christmas.

Sincerely, your friend,
Bill

I left the letter on his desk, but he never came in that Thursday. He actually never came into work again. His wife and fourteen-year-old son came home that evening and there he lay on the kitchen floor. He had a heart attack and died. All the warnings signs were there, but he did not want to help himself. Those of us who knew him best watched him slowly commit suicide by ignoring and not wanting to help his situation.

It pains me to think that he never read the letter that I wrote, but it may not have been intended for him. Maybe it's for you or someone you love.

This was the second time in three years that our department lost someone. It is not an easy process, but we coped with it the best we knew how. For me, this was preparation for watching yet someone else die, someone very close to me, and the worst was yet to come.

CHAPTER 10

The Move

My good friend, the one who got into that scuffle with those kids at the shore, was now a proud papa himself and actually celebrated the birth of his son around the same time we were celebrating the birth of my son. We jokingly said, "Look out, world, another generation of us!" We could only hope that our kids would not make the same mistakes we did. Though life had its ups, it certainly had its fair share of downs, because he then found out that his mother was slowly dying from cancer.

She and I were pretty close. We had known each other for a very long time since her son and I went to high school together. I don't think there was a prouder person at her son's wedding to see me standing up there officiating the wedding. She knew how far I had come, where I had been, and where I was now, and she knew that if I could change, God's power was available to anyone and everyone who believed.

She had been through a lot in life, losing her husband when both of her sons were relatively young. She had met her husband when he was stationed in the army in Germany, and she left everything she knew behind to come to America and start her own family with him. They were young, in love, and ready to conquer the world together.

She had a lot to be proud of. She was an exceptional mother, a great friend, and a pleasure to be around. She touched each and every person that she met in a very positive way. This is why when she approached me and asked me to do her funeral when she died, I considered it a great honor and a blessing, and I gladly said yes.

We sat down on numerous occasions together to discuss details on how she wanted it to go. She was a believer, and she just knew she was going to a better place, which really strengthened my faith as I did my best to strengthen hers. She wanted the funeral to be uplifting and more of a life celebration.

As time went on, her health declined, and she was placed on hospice care. Her family and close friends were by her side, and even family from Germany flew out to be with her. It broke my heart to see her mother watch as she slowly lost her daughter. She could not speak English very well, but you could see the love and pain in her eyes.

I would see her in person, call her on the phone, and kept her in my prayers daily. One evening, as I was driving home from work, I just felt led to pull over to the side of the road and give her a call. I spoke with her and told her that I felt like I needed to pray for her. This would be the last time I had a conversation with her while she was coherent, and the last words I spoke to her were, "I love you."

The following week, her son called me and said that the hospice nurse said that she did not have much time left. They were thinking that she would be gone within a week. He wanted to know if I wanted to come over and spend some time with her before she died. I told him that I would be over first thing in the morning.

I showed up with coffee and donuts early the following morning t. My friend as well as his brother and his mother's mother were there. I asked if I could be alone with her for a few minutes, and they said, "No problem." Her mother stayed in the room and watched from a distance as I sat in a chair across from her.

As she lay there, I could sense that her spirit was ready to leave her body. It is a tough feeling to explain, but I just felt it. I told her that when she was willing, to let her spirit go home and be with the Lord. I told her that her days as a pilgrim on earth had come to an end, and she was now ready to go to a place where there was no more pain and no more suffering to be at rest and at peace. I whispered that she was loved by many, had touched so many people, and that her earthly journey was drawing to a close. I told her that she had much to be proud of, but her work here was finished. She did not have to hang on any longer, and when she was ready, to go and be with Jesus. I anointed her with some oil, in the name of the Father, and of the Son, and of the Holy Spirit. I prayed once more for her, told her she was an exceptional mother, and when she felt it was time to go home, to give her spirit up.

At that very moment, I put my hand on her forehead, gave her a kiss, and told her that I loved her. A tear, trickled down from her eye, she smiled, and I looked over at her mother as she watched everything unfold before her very eyes. I could not communicate with her because I could not speak German, but I went over to her, held her hand, told her that her daughter was at peace and would be going home soon.

I left the room and went into the kitchen to be with my friend and his brother. A neighbor then arrived to go see her. She sat down and then said we needed to get in there as soon as we could because she was gone.

I'll never forget that day, because I had never experienced death as beautifully as I just had. It was very touching to see the family come together and mourn their loss. My friend and his brother, their children, their grandmother, friends, and family all came together to support one another. Before we knew it, there was a house full of support. The hospice nurse took charge and asked if we all wanted to come around her, hold hands, and say the Lord's Prayer.

It was very touching and more like a homecoming. I was very much moved, and although I did not want to see her go, I knew she was in a better place. My friend said that she must have been waiting for me to die and asked what I said to her. I told him all that had transpired, and it was a very beautiful moment.

About a week later, I gave the funeral, and I do believe that it brought closure for every one there. I even found someone about a week before who could take everything that I was going to say and translate it into German. I think the most gratifying part of the service for me was to give a copy of everything that I was going to say to a mother who had just lost her daughter. There were others there as well who had just flown in from Germany, could not speak English, and I had plenty of copies to go around. She will be missed greatly, but I know that she is with Jesus, which as the Bible states, "is far better."

I loved what I did. I offered hope to a lost and dying world, and the answer was Jesus. If only my dad could understand this!

I went to see him almost daily, maybe just for a few minutes after work, and sometimes a few hours on the weekend, and I was starting to notice a real change in him. He was getting slower, off balance, and he was not walking Ralph. He had a letter on his counter stating that someone had called the condo association complaining that his backyard smelled like a kennel. I went outside and I could see why. You can't let a big, black Labrador go to the bathroom in a tiny area and never clean it up. The following weekend I cleaned it all up and had four big garbage bags filled with mulch and dog feces.

He was going out a lot, doing his own thing, and spending a lot of time at the casino. As much as I hated to see him go, he really loved it there, and he was treated like a VIP. He got a lot of attention from the staff there, and he was starting to make some friends. I would have rather seen him make friends with people at another location and spend his time elsewhere, but he just was not interested. I was praying constantly for him, discussed all types of hobby possibilities, but he just did not want to do anything else. And then he hit it big playing slots and won fifty thousand dollars not once but actually two times! I could not believe it.

I knew things were not going to get any better with my dad, and I also knew that he did not like living alone. I talked it over with my wife, and we were planning to look for a new house closer to her work. I said to her, "Why don't we propose the idea to Dad and see if he wants to go in on a house with an in-law suite? This way he can be as independent as he wants, I can take care of Ralph, he won't be alone, and more importantly, I can keep my eye on him. I really think his health is getting worse, and it would be good for him to always have someone around."

It took a little convincing, but she decided it was a good idea. I talked it over with my dad, and he said, "Let's do it."

After a few months of looking at houses, we finally found a place in Chalfont, PA. It was nice and close to my wife's work, but farther for me to travel back and forth to Princeton, NJ, every day. Sometimes in life you make sacrifices for the ones you love.

We put our house up for sale, and so did my dad. We both sold our houses pretty quickly, but unfortunately, my wife and I took a hit on ours and lost money, but such is life. We also now had the challenge of trying to find a new church home. Finding a new church should be just as an important and a meticulous process as looking for a new house. You cannot just settle for anything, and there are a lot of churches that just will not make the cut.

When we finally moved in, my dad seemed a bit happier in general, which was good to see. However, he picked up the habit of smoking cigarettes again, I think out of sheer boredom. If he did not go the casino or have anything planned for the day, he would spend most of the day napping, watching television, or playing solitaire. I did what I could to get him interested in something or anything, even gave him plenty of reading materials, but his constant claim was that he was too busy, which he always said in his comical way. The fact of the matter is that he hated to read, admitted that he was lazy, and just did not want to do anything.

It was about mid-September, and my wife had just called me at work around six thirty and told me that I was not going to believe what happened. I needed to brace myself, because as comical as it may sound, this was going to be the start of constant worry about my dad. Apparently, he had gotten up in the morning sometime around ten o'clock to go to the bathroom. After he was finished, he decided to go outside and have a cigarette. Since it was in the backyard, and nobody would see him, he figured he would just go out in his pajama gear, which consisted of a pair of boxers, no shirt, and a pair of socks. It was a little chilly out, so he decided to make it quick, but he had accidentally locked the door behind him, left his cell phone inside, and had no way to get back in.

He did not know what to do at this point. He did not want to look like the crazy guy in just a pair of boxers and start knocking on neighbors' doors to ask if he could use their phone. The only thing he could think to do was to break the door window and go in. He took the chair that he was sitting on and threw it a few times to break the glass. Unfortunately for him, the glass was too thick, and he could not break it. He also tried to do the same thing to our glass doors on the patio, but once it again it was a failed attempt.

He was now getting cold, and the only place he could go was to the back shed. He went inside, sat in a chair, took some old blankets, and kept himself warm. He said he heard people walking by all day, school buses, and children, but he just did not know how to call out for help. He knew that my wife got home around six thirty, so he figured his only option was to wait it out until she got home and then she could let him in.

He waited outside in his boxers and his socks, in the cold, in the shed, for eight hours! Around six thirty, he watched the house, the lights came on, and finally she let the dogs out. He then went to the back door, and she said it was a sight to see. There was my dad freezing cold in his boxers!

She immediately did what she could to warm him up by getting some clean blankets, some clothes, and hot soup.

Now this may sound comical, which in fact it was, but it was also scary at the same time. I could not have going forward taken the chance of this happening again or thinking about what else could happen. I know this was an accidental occurrence, but to have a man in his seventies outside all day in his underwear was not okay. He made jokes about it though and said at least he had smokes. No doubt, from there on out, he took his cell phone wherever he went, and if he went outside, he put on some clothes. But this was only the beginning to his accidental shenanigans.

In time, we noticed other things that were not like him. We noticed that his car had dents, dings, and scratches more and more as he went out. There was also noticeable damage to the walls and objects around his space in the garage, and they matched up to some of the minor damages to his car. When I questioned him about it, he was either in denial or did not remember. He also had scratches, cuts, and bruises on obvious parts of his body, like his head, arms, and legs, and when we asked him about them, he would say that he did not know or could not remember.

I was really tempted to start hiding his keys from him so he couldn't drive, but he would never forgive me. I asked him if he thought he was capable of driving anymore and obviously he took it very personal and said of course he was.

When he went to the casino, he would leave around ten o'clock at night and not come home until eight in the morning. I knew in that duration he was drinking wine, and I felt like the roles were reversed and I was his father now always in a constant state of worry, calling him all the time to make sure he was okay. My biggest worry was that he would not only hurt himself but innocent bystanders on the road.

At the time, my youngest sister was not working, and she came over a lot with her son to spend time with him during the day. She even helped him out going food shopping, went to doctor appointments with him, and basically did whatever he wanted to do. They had lots of good times together, and it was a good bonding experience for them, but she had her hands full. Just going to the grocery store with him, out to lunch, dinner, or anywhere in general turned into some kind of big production because he always had to be the center of attention, and you always knew that if there was an attractive woman present, he would make an outrageous statement to her that would make both the woman and whoever Dad was with uncomfortable.

She then brought to my attention that she thought he was starting to have issues with his bladder and bowels because she was starting to notice that he did not make it to the bathroom in time. If he had an accident, he would do his best to cover it up in some way or just ignore it like it did not happen. In time, his underwear, shorts, and pants began to end up missing. We knew that he was throwing them in the garbage, and we thought that he was driving the materials to a public garbage can so we would never know.

This became apparent one day when my sister's fiancé's father died. We all went to the funeral. My wife and I drove in one car, and we brought my dad. On the way there, an interesting conversation developed between me, my wife, and my dad.

I said, "Although it pains me that we are going to a funeral, and my thoughts and prayers go out to the son who lost his father, it gives me great joy knowing that he was a Christian and he is now with Jesus. The body that we see before us today is just that, a body, and we can be assured that his soul is now with Jesus, and there is no better place to be."

My dad said, "That is your belief and not mine; how do you know that there is even a God?"

My wife said, "If there was no God, then Jesus's claims are all wrong. Do you believe in Jesus?"

My dad said, "I'm sure that Jesus was around a long time ago, but I don't see how somebody can know that there is a God."

I said, "Is that your belief or just a general belief?"

My dad said, "I don't think anyone can really know that God exists—I mean, I don't know."

I said, "Okay, now we are getting somewhere. So you classify yourself as an agnostic. I understand now, and that makes some sense to me."

He said, "Agnostic? Well, I don't like the sound of that."

I said, "Well, that is what being an agnostic is. It is the belief that one cannot know for sure if God exists, so therefore you are an agnostic."

He said, "Well, I don't know if He does or doesn't."

I said, "Well, you in general or humankind cannot know? There are two different brackets to agnosticism. Either you personally can't or everyone can't. Where do you fall?

He said, "Well, even if He did, I don't want to know."

I said, "Oh, okay, now this makes sense. You now fall in the category of a willingly ignorant agnostic."

My dad said, "Ignorant? That was not a very nice thing to say to me. And here you call yourself a Christian?"

I said, "I am speaking the truth. You just flat out admitted that even if God existed, you don't even want to know. You said it, not me. Did you hear it, babe?"

My wife said, "Yeah, I heard it."

I said, "This is a very dangerous place to be, Dad. Even if I provided you with evidence for God, you plainly admit that you don't want to know. Think about it."

My dad said, "Whatever. Are we almost there?"

He then changed the subject. I knew as well as he did that he did not mean what he said. He just liked to cause controversy, and since he did not like where the conversation was headed, he changed the subject.

When the funeral was over, I asked my dad if he had to go to the bathroom before we left, and he said he would go and try.

My wife and I were waiting outside, everyone was gone, and it was a half hour later. I decided to go in to see if he was all right. I opened up the restroom door, and there was an obvious trail that showed he had not made it to the stall.

I wanted to do what I could to help and asked him if he was all right without embarrassing him. He told me everything was fine and to go outside and wait for him. He was in there for another half hour trying to clean himself up and then finally came out.

My wife and I knew what had happened because in the car there was a really bad odor because it was all over his clothes. I knew that as a loving son, I had to confront him about it and do what I could to help him but do my best not to embarrass him.

I finally manned up that night and had a heart-to-heart with him. I told him that although he might be embarrassed about it, it was a situation that could be helped, and he should talk to his doctor about it, and it was all just a part of life. In the meantime, I gave him a box of adult diapers, put them in his drawer, and told him that they would be in there if he ever felt he needed them, especially for when he went out. It would save him the embarrassment if he had an accident, and no one had to know about it.

As I went up the stairs, I'll never forget the look on his face. With a tear in his eye, he said, "Thank you, son."

It broke my heart to see him in such a humbling stage of life. They say, "You come into the world in diapers and you leave the world in them too." Here was the guy, my father, who used to change my diapers when I was a baby, and now here I was returning the favor to him as an old man. But I would do anything for that man, and his pride was starting to subside, and he realized that he was not as independent that he used to be, and he needed help. That is why I took the liberty to move in with him—I just did not think it was going to happen so quickly.

It was nice to see him every day, especially when I got home. If I wanted to see him, I did not have to call him—I could just walk down the stairs to see how he was doing. I still tried my best to talk about spiritual things, but he would change the subject immediately. He was a man who had money, and in his mind, he didn't need anything else. He did what he wanted whenever he wanted to do it, and that temporarily made him happy, but it was a fleeting feeling, and he knew that it would go away, so he constantly kept doing more to try to get that feeling back.

Life went on as usual for a while, and then I had another great moment to build a believer up in the faith in the most unexpected place.

We had just recently moved in, and my doctor made an appointment for me to get some bloodwork done. I made an appointment for a Saturday.

I went in and the nurse took me to the office and took my blood pressure. She said that it was very high for someone my age. I told her that was the reason I was there; we were looking for options to get it controlled, and I was more than likely going to be going on medication. High blood pressure ran in my family, and I was not eating right, not exercising anymore, and the stress I had been under was not helping the situation.

I was sitting there getting a needle in my arm, and the nurse said to me, "You know, for some reason I feel like I can talk to you."

I said, "Believe it or not, this happens from time to time. Is everything all right?"

She then began to pour her heart out to me.

She said, "I just recently found out that my husband had been unfaithful, and I am having problems coping with the situation."

I said, "Are you a Christian?"

She said, "I am, and so is my husband."

I said, "Are you willing to try to make the marriage work?"

She said, "As hard as it may be, I am."

I sat there with her as she cried and told me just about everything. I counseled and consoled her using biblical methods of forgiveness. I told her it was not a sign of weakness but a sign of strength to reach out for help. I told her that an unfaithful spouse is probably one of the hardest things to cope with as a Christian, but forgiveness was possible.

She thanked me for my time and said that she felt a lot better. She said that she was also going to look for help through her church.

A week later, I stopped in and saw her behind the counter. She ran over to me and gave me a hug. She said that things were getting a lot better, she and her husband started counseling sessions with her pastor, and I was so happy to hear that.

I told her that I stopped in to give her a gift. I gave her two books. One on forgiving an unfaithful spouse as a Christian, and the other one she could read together with her husband entitled, *The Love Dare*. I told her that they were gifts, and I had never seen someone so happy before in my life. She said there I was just coming into get bloodwork done and I had touched her life and was part of saving her marriage. She said that God worked in some awesome ways.

I said, "You have no idea!"

CHAPTER 11

Life Is Fleeting

After officiating forty-seven weddings, in the middle of April 2015, I decided it was time to take a break. I took my ministry off of wedding sites and put the word out that I was done doing them. Whether or not I would ever do anymore in the future, I did not know, but with the time available, I was going to be able to focus in more on my personal studies, or actually, unbeknown to me at the time, God needed me to focus my attention elsewhere.

Don't get me wrong, I loved to do weddings, but they did take up a lot of my time, and I just felt led to take a break. You will see why shortly.

It was starting to become very obvious that my dad's health was slowly declining. My little sister kept me posted on the outcome of his doctor appointments, and nothing was ever reported that was life-threatening, but his doctor strongly encouraged him to start walking and stop smoking again at the very least.

We did our best to encourage him to do that. We even tried to sell it to him in a positive way. We told him that he did not have to walk around the block in the cold; he could go to the mall and look at the good-looking women that were there to walk around too. We could even go as far as get him a treadmill, and he could walk while he watched television. He did not take our advice, and he had trouble putting on his shoes one day. He was with my little sister, and it turned out that his feet and legs were swollen.

They went to the hospital because he was off balance and did not feel good. It took a lot for him to go the hospital, so we knew that it was serious.

The doctors drained his legs, the swelling went down, and he was home the next day. This unfortunately was a sign of things to come.

About two months later, on June 5, I was at work and my wife called me. She said that Dad was not looking good, his legs and feet were very swollen again, and he would not go to the hospital. My little sister was there too trying to persuade him to go, but he just would not give in. I told them I would be home in a little while, and I would talk to him.

My sister called me on my cell phone on my way home from work and said she was very worried about him. She said that he had fallen down a couple of times, and his legs looked a lot worse than the last time. She said that for some reason he listens to me, and I needed to get him to go to the hospital. I told her that I would get him to go.

I got home and walked down to his apartment. He was sitting in his chair, sleeping, and the television was on. He had his shoes and socks off and was wearing a pair of jeans with a button-down short-sleeve shirt.

He looked very pale, and I said, "Dad, wake up. Come on, what are you doing? You really don't look too good. How do you feel?"

He said, "I'm fine, why is everybody so worried about me? I'm fine. This will go away."

I said, "No, it won't. Things like this just don't go away on their own. You need medical attention. You don't look well, and let me look at your legs. Your feet are swollen!"

I bent down to lift up his pant leg so I could look at his legs, but his pants were so tight I could not get them to pull up at all.

I said, "Dad, unbutton your pants. Pull your pants down; I want to see your legs."

He said, "No. I'm fine. Let me watch this show."

I said, "Come on, Dad. Please. This really is serious."

He said, "Fine."

As he stood up, he almost fell down, but I caught him. I held him up as he unbuttoned his pants and then pulled them down. They got stuck right below his knee, and I made him sit.

I pulled each pant leg off very carefully, and his pants were soaked because as I pulled the pants down, his legs began to leak fluid.

I said, "Dad, look at your legs. They are not just swollen, but you are leaking fluid! We have to get you to a hospital."

He said, "No, I am fine. I'll just wait it out."

I said, "Just wait it out? Look, either you are coming with me, or I am calling an ambulance. I am not taking no for an answer. You are going to the hospital one way or another."

I then walked into his bedroom and bathroom, packed a bag for him, got some sweatpants, put them on him, and helped him up.

He said, "Promise me I am going to come back here tonight. I really don't want to leave."

I said, "I know, Dad. I can't promise you anything though because I don't know what is going to happen. I'll do my best to get you back here as soon as I can, okay?"

He said, "Good enough for me."

We then walked out to my car. It was a very slow process because he was so off balance.

I called my three sisters one by one to tell them what was going on. My two younger sisters were on their way to the hospital, but my older sister was in Georgia, so I told her I would keep her posted.

I said to my dad, "What are you doing? There are so many people that love and care about you. You nearly gave your daughter-in-law and your daughter a heart attack. They don't want to see anything happen to you. Why do you have to be so stubborn? Just because you don't want to deal with something does not make it go away. I love you, I don't want to see you like this, and in all seriousness, do you even want to get better?"

He said, "Of course I do. They will just drain my legs, give me some pills, and then I'll be on my way. My doctor said the last time I saw him that he gives me another ten good years to live, but after that, I was on my own."

I said, "Dad, doctors can be wrong. That is only his opinion, and you certainly are not helping the situation by picking up smoking again, not exercising, and living the way that you do. You are like a cat, but you have more than nine lives! But the fact of the matter is that you only get one life to live. You are mortal! You have cheated death more than anyone I have ever known. You have had strokes, an aneurism, and even beat cancer, and look at you right now, you are even smoking a cigarette! For someone who does not believe in God, I am convinced you are a living example of what the Bible says in 2 Peter 3:9: 'The Lord is not slack concerning his promise, as some men count slackness; but is longsuffering to us-ward, not willing that any should perish, but that all should come to repentance.'"

He said, "I don't know about all that, but°…"

I said, "No buts about it. Your life is just so precious, and God loves you so much. I have seen the incredible things He has done in your life, and I praise Him every day for it. He has blessed you far more than you give Him credit for; in fact, you don't give Him any credit whatsoever! It's like you are blind and cannot see it! God is longsuffering, patient, slow to anger, abounds in love, and is keeping you around so you will not perish without Him. It is your choice though. You are just so stubborn and hard-hearted, I just wish you would see it, but God is not going to make you love Him. If you want Him, He is there with His arms wide open waiting for you."

He said, "All right, let's not get crazy about this. I'm not dying or anything. They are just going to drain my legs and give me some more pills to take, and that will be it. Back to normal, you'll see."

I said, "Normal? There is no normal with you, Dad. You are running out of chances, you are running out of your cat lives, and before you know it, there won't be a pill that can help you anymore. I just love you so much and°…"

He said, "I love you too. Let's just get to the hospital so I can get home and go to bed. I'm really tired."

I pulled up by the emergency room doors. I ran inside and got a wheelchair. My dad wanted to have one more cigarette before he went in, so he had one sitting in the wheelchair while I went to park the car.

My two younger sisters pulled up, and we all went inside at the same time as I pushed my dad in the wheelchair. They admitted him to the emergency room, and it was a very long night. They gave him a Xanax that he kept asking for, and he finally fell asleep. They took x-rays and all kinds of tests and said that he was going to be there for the night and possibly tomorrow.

My little sister and I decided to leave, and my other sister stayed with him, telling us that she would keep us posted.

The following day I went to the hospital, and he scheduled to undergo an operation. He was to have a thoracentesis-plural infusion, where they were basically going to go in through his back with a large suction-like device and drain the fluid that was building up around his lungs.

He was very scared and was coming to realize that this was a lot more serious than he thought. To top it off, the operation did not go as according to plan, and afterwards they gave us the worst news you could possibly want to hear.

On June 7, two days after he was admitted through the emergency room for what my dad thought was going to be an in and out procedure, the physicians concluded, very empathetically, that there was nothing more they could do for him.

He was said to be at his end stage in life and was diagnosed with advanced congestive heart failure, advanced COPD (chronic obstructive pulmonary disease, which was likely caused by smoking cigarettes), and there was also possible internal bleeding as well as chronic AFib (atrial fibrillation.) He was on daily Lasix, and because of all the fluid retention and his refusal to quit smoking cigarettes, nothing would ever get better. It would just be a constant cycle with or without smoking; the damage was done. The only option going forward was palliative care (keeping him comfortable and without pain). There would be no more doctor appointments, procedures, specialists, new medications, or pills. The end of his life was drawing near.

We were all very saddened by the news, and my dad had trouble coming to the realization that he was going to die. He did not like not being in charge of a situation and coming to grips with all of this was too much for him. He was very upset over the news and said that if he was the president of the United States they would be able to fix him somehow. The reality was that the president took care of himself and my father did not. My sisters who were there were very saddened by this news, as was I, but I was more concerned about his eternal destination. I wanted and needed for him to be responsive to the gospel. I had tried the best that I could ever since I had become a Christian, but now it was of the utmost importance to me. But would he now finally listen?

Life as we knew it had changed forever, and now every moment with him was very precious. I had to become a prayer warrior. You cannot go anywhere in life as a Christian without prayer. This is where I began, and I needed God's direction in what to do next. This was the beginning of me and my dad's road together of intense spiritual and very emotional conversations.

CHAPTER 12

Tick Tock

I called my older sister in Georgia to give her the news about the situation. No one likes to be the bearer of bad news, but someone had to tell her. On June 9, she took a flight with her husband from Georgia to Philadelphia, rented a car, and drove to St. Mary's Hospital in Newtown, Pennsylvania, where my dad was.

I called my boss and notified him of the situation. He had known my dad for many years and told me to take as much time as I needed. Not only was he a great boss, but I truly valued our friendship. I don't know what I would have done without his patience, understanding, and above all compassion and love. To call him a friend would be an understatement—he was a brother who I would lay down my life for, and I loved him dearly.

The next couple of days it felt like time had stopped. I felt like I was in the twilight zone. He had lots of visitors, but someone kept sneaking him cigarettes, and he was smoking in the bathroom on a hospital floor that had oxygen and was reprimanded for it. The last thing we wanted to see was the whole floor blow up killing many innocent people all because he wanted a cigarette. We all spent as much time as we could with him, but we all had our lives, jobs, and family to attend to. Still, he had an awesome support system, he was loved very much, and not for a moment was he alone.

My older sister did not leave his side. She and her husband then flew back to Georgia and were going to try and figure out what they could do next. My brother-in-law worked for an airline, my older sister was a school teacher, and she was drawing very close to her time off for the summer.

We all decided the best option for him was to be admitted to Rock Hill Mennonite Nursing Home in the rehabilitation part of the facility. This is where his father (Poppy) and stepmother (Gummy) spent the remaining days of their lives. This is also where they could keep him comfortable, work on physical rehab, and take it day by day to come up with a plan going forward. Though there was no hope for him to fully recover, we wanted to keep him alive as long as possible and comfortable, but he would have to want to work the program, and it would take physical work, which he would not be up for.

The only problem was that he could not be discharged until June 12, which now was two long days away. In a hospital setting, time goes very slowly, and two days feels like two weeks sitting in the same room.

They kept him at the hospital and did their best to keep him comfortable. He had a twenty-four hour breathing tube so he could get the oxygen he needed. The staff would also make sure he was eating right, and taking the pills that he had been taking before he went in. He also now would have to use a BIPAP (Bilevel Positive Airway Pressure) machine and wear a mask while he slept. This was a breathing apparatus that helped get more air into his lungs, which my dad desperately needed. It would not get him better, but it would help him tremendously.

This was all happening so fast, and he was having a lot of difficulty coming to terms with the situation. I would imagine that anyone in his place would be in the same mind-set.

After all his visitors had left, I decided to stay the night with him so we could have some much needed alone time, and I wanted to hear where he was mentally and, more importantly, spiritually. I believed in my heart that it was time to talk about it on a serious but loving level.

He was sleeping, and I was sitting in a chair next to his bed reading the book of Job. I loved the book of Job. It truly was one of my favorite books in the Bible and possibly the oldest as well. It was a thinking person's book. In my opinion, no other book addressed the issue of suffering better, and I think it was the book that I read the most in the Bible.

Here was a guy who had everything taken away from him. He lost his possessions, children, and even his health all in a matter of days. He suffered so much, and God considered him "blameless and upright, a man who feared God, and shunned evil." Job's wife tells him to "curse God and just die," and all the while he's getting advice from his three "wise" friends that did not pertain to Job and his situation. Job never blamed God for his trial, he only had questions, and above all, he still trusted Him. If only Job knew the reason why he was going through what he was going through. As the reader, we know, but he did not. There is a lot to learn from this book, but I think the wisest thing we can learn is that although we suffer in this life, we must understand that God still loves us. We must in return love God whether we are experiencing suffering or blessings while we prepare for eternal life where there is no more suffering and only blessings.

The wisest thing that Job's three friends did was sit with him for seven days and seven nights without saying a word because they saw how great his suffering was. This was based on an ancient Jewish tradition that when people came to comfort someone, they would not say anything until the person who is suffering speaks.

This really is a wise tradition because all too often people end up speaking too soon and giving bad advice even though they think it's good. Now, here my dad lay going through the trial of his life, but he did not have and know God, and he felt alone.

For my dad, being alone was the most fearful situation he could ever face in life. I wanted to help, but I needed to be careful not to say the wrong things like Job's friends did. They may have had good intentions, but they were clearly wrong. I also wanted to have the right answers for him if he had questions about God. I decided to wait for him and prayed that God would soften his heart through the experience he was enduring.

He finally woke up, looked around the room, and said, "Where is everybody, and what time is it?"

I said, "It's ten o'clock. They all left, and I told them that I would stay with you tonight. Is that all right?"

He said, "Sure, son."

I said, "Listen, Dad. I can't empathize with what you are going through mentally, but I am here for you. We are all here for you. I love you very much."

He said, "All I know is that if I were the president of the United States, they would be able to fix me."

I said, "Dad, in all honesty, the president is not seventy-six years old, has not been diagnosed with advanced congestive heart failure, advanced COPD, chronic AFib, does not have possible internal bleeding, is not on daily Lasix, and does not have fluid retention like you. The president takes care of himself; you unfortunately have not. You did what you wanted whenever you wanted, ate what you wanted whenever you wanted, drank whatever you wanted whenever you wanted, smoked when you wanted, and did not exercise. The president I'm sure has a healthy diet, exercises, does not smoke two packs a cigarettes a day, and he is many years younger than you. You are on two entirely different ends of the spectrum in life. I wish this was not the case, but we have to look at your situation for what it is, as sad as it may be."

He said, "Well, if he were in my shoes, you bet they would have a new heart for him within an hour!"

I said, "Is that what this is about? A new heart?"

He said, "If I could get a new one of those, everything would be fine."

I said, "Dad, in all honesty, think about what you are saying. I understand that you are upset, but you are in no condition to get a heart transplant. First and foremost, undergoing that kind of surgery at your age and with how fragile your body is would kill you. Any type of surgery now, due to your condition, would kill you. Doctors would not take that chance and perform an operation like that!"

He said, "Well, why not just try, I'm going to die anyway! If I were the president, it wouldn't kill me. They would do everything to keep him alive."

I said, "I love you, Dad, but it really has nothing to do with you being the president. As old and fragile as you are, and with the limited amount of heart donors there are in the world, a heart transplant is out of the question for you."

He said, "Well, if I were the president, I would have a new heart."

I said, "Well, you are not the president."

He said, "I know that, but if I was, I would be fine."

I said, "So we need to deal with this for what it is. I think that you can say that I know you pretty well, would you agree?"

He said, "Yeah, I agree you know me pretty good."

I said, "Well, let's just say you were cleared to undergo a major operation such as a heart transplant. Do you know how long a wait is to get one? Do you understand what kind of list of people are waiting for one?"

He said, "No. Do you?"

I said, "Statistically, I'll be honest, I really don't know, but I am sure it is very long. There are many people ahead of you, and just getting you on a list like that probably isn't an easy thing to do. So let's say you get on this list; it could take many months or maybe years to find a match. Plus, even when the operation happened, there is not a one hundred percent chance that it would go perfectly, even if the operation was a success. The new heart would have to try to adapt to your body, and I am sure that is no easy task. Would you then begin to take care of yourself with a proper diet, exercise, do what the doctors tell you to do, and quit smoking? In all honesty?"

He stared at the wall with a blank look. About a minute later, breaking a really uncomfortable silence in the room, he said, "Probably not."

I said, "So you have hundreds or maybe even thousands of people on this list patiently waiting and praying for a donor in hospitals all over the country. They are all waiting for a heart they would do anything to have, and they would take care of themselves if they got a new heart and a new chance to live. All types of people too—young men, women, and even children who are in this very sad situation for various depressing reasons. You would be willing, hypothetically speaking, take a new heart from Peggy Sue, who is fourteen years old, who has her entire life ahead of her, and would take care of herself? I am just throwing around a possibility. Or how about Jimmy Jones, who is twenty and got into a major car accident, needs a heart as soon as possible, and would live the rest of his life more grateful for it than you?"

He said, "Well, I did not look at it that way."

I said, "Well, you know we're just talking hypothetically, but they are possibilities. No one is more special than anyone, we are all made in the image of God, and all life is precious to Him, but situations arise in life where important decisions need to be made. I know that if I were in your shoes, if a heart did become available and it could go to a kid rather than me with his or her entire life ahead of him or her, I would give the heart to the kid because I know where I am going when I take my last breath. I know it is easier said than done, but would you?"

He sat there with a very serious look on his face, staring at the wall for a good two minutes, and did not say a word. He then sat up in his bed and said, "If I could get a new heart, you are probably right. I would not take care of myself. I don't know how many more years I would have left if I did get a new one, but I know that if it did go to a kid, they would get more out of it than me."

I said, "Even if you were the president?"

He said, "Yeah."

I said, "All I know is that I love you, God loves you, I am here for you, and if you want to talk about anything, I'm here."

He said, "God? Huh."

I said, "Yes, God. You know, the one who if He existed you really would not want to know Him anyway, right?"

He said, "I never said that. I think that there just might be someone in charge up there, but He is not doing a very good job."

I said, "Well, maybe your train of thought has changed since your circumstances have changed, and if you want to talk about it, I'm here for you."

He said, "My son, the priest."

I said, "Dad, I am not a priest."

He said, "Well, I suppose that you think you have all the answers, right?"

I said, "No. I know I don't have all the answers. I probably have more questions than you do, but the difference between you and me is that I believe in a God who loves me, and I know where I am going to go when I die."

He said, "You don't know that. Nobody knows that. No one has ever died and come back to tell about it!"

This was the moment I had been waiting for°…

I said, "This is where you are wrong. I know someone who has in fact died and came back to tell His story. If there was someone who made that claim, wouldn't you want to know more?"

He said, "Of course, but I would be very skeptical about it."

I said, "And you should. Not everybody can make a claim like that, but I know someone who predicted He was going to die and then three days later would rise from the dead. This someone also said that all who believed in Him would live forever in a place where there was no more pain and suffering and be in a constant state of joy. Wouldn't you want to go to a place like that after you die?"

He said, "Sure I would, if only it were true. I suppose this someone you are talking about is Jesus?"

I said, "It sure is."

He said, "So He actually predicted that He was going to die and then be resurrected, huh?"

I said, "Yes. He actually said the time frame too—in three days. This is remarkable, and all four Gospels report it. For instance (I grabbed my Bible and turned to Mark), listen here. In Mark eight thirty-one it says, 'And He began to teach them, that the Son of man must suffer many things, and be rejected of the elders, and of the chief priests, and scribes, and be killed, and after three days rise again.' That is pretty powerful, isn't it, Dad?"

He said, "Look, I don't want to do a Bible study. How do you even know that Jesus said that? This could all be made up. There just is no proof. If there was a God, why doesn't He just prove it to me and everyone else who don't believe?"

I said, "Dad, you really are asking good questions, and there are good answers as long as you are willing to listen. Are you?"

He then got very quiet again and began to look at the wall in front of him with a blank stare. After about a minute, I said, "Would you be willing to really listen?"

He said, "Yeah, sure."

I said, "Well you know Jesus dealt with people who were skeptical in His day too. He was going all over performing miracles, making the deaf hear, the blind see, raising the dead, all kinds of awesome stuff, but He still had opposition. Some people, even some that were close to Him, did not believe what He was doing. But He still pointed to His resurrection as the icing on the cake to validate His divinity.

You cannot just predict your death and resurrection from the dead without God being involved."

He said, "Oh, yeah. How do we know that He really rose from the dead? I want proof."

I said, "I am not sure what kind of proof you are looking for. It is not like I can run out and grab a DVD and show you a video that someone recorded of the event that happened over two thousand years ago. But I can tell you that even Paul said that if Jesus did not rise from the dead, the Christian faith would be worthless.

I grabbed my Bible and turned to 1 Corinthians.

I said, "I know you don't want to do a Bible study, but just listen to this. Paul said this: 'But if there be no resurrection of the dead, then is Christ not risen: And if Christ be not risen, then is our preaching vain, and your faith is also vain. Yea, and we are found false witnesses of God; because we have testified of God that he raised up Christ: whom he raised not up, if so be that the dead rise not. For if the dead rise not, then is not Christ raised: And if Christ be not raised, your faith is vain; ye are yet in your sins'"(1 Corinthians 15:13–17).

He said, "So?"

I said, "So he then goes on to say that our faith is *not* worthless in: "If in this life only we have hope in Christ, we are of all men most miserable. But now is Christ risen from the dead, and become the firstfruits of them that slept."

(1 Corinthians 15:19-20) So, Dad, Jesus rose from the dead; we can have confidence of this as hard as it maybe to believe! So what kind of proof are you looking for Dad?"

He said, "Well, proof within reason. I'll grant that you can't give me a DVD."

I said, "Okay, what you must realize is that after Jesus was crucified and buried, three days later His body went missing."

He said, "Well, how do you know it was not stolen?"

I said, "By whom?"

He said, "I don't know, just someone."

I said, "Well, first we would have look at motive. You were in the DEA, so you should know that. Who would want to do that? The Jews or Romans wouldn't because then they would be able to shut the Christians up by producing Jesus's body since Christians were proclaiming that He rose from the dead. It was actually an early circulated rumor that the disciples stole the body. The Bible even says that.

I grabbed my Bible again, turned to **Matthew 28:11–15**, and read out loud: "Now when they were going, behold, some of the watch came into the city, and shewed unto the chief priests all the things that were done. And when they were assembled with the elders, and had taken counsel, they gave large money unto the soldiers, Saying, Say ye, His disciples came by night, and stole him away while we slept.

And if this come to the governor's ears, we will persuade him, and secure you. So they took the money, and did as they were taught: and this saying is commonly reported among the Jews until this day."

He said, "Well, what if it was true, and it wasn't a rumor?"

I said, "Highly unlikely and still there is no motive. Plus, the disciples were scared and did not know what to do next without Jesus; two of them had even left town. They also would have had to roll away the rock from the tomb while it was guarded by Jewish guards or Roman guards, or maybe even both, while they were asleep, which was an offense punishable by death. Then, on top of that, would most of the disciples willingly be martyred knowing that the resurrection was a lie? It is kind of ridiculous if you think about it, isn't it? The tomb being guarded also squashes the possibility of some random thief stealing Jesus's body."

He said, "Yeah, well, maybe Jesus was not dead."

I said, "Okay, now this is what is commonly known as the swoon theory, but it really does not hold up."

He said, "Yeah, why is that?"

I said, "First, you have to remember that Jesus was flogged and was in critical condition even before He was crucified. Historians have discovered that there were many people who died from flogging even before they had the chance to be crucified. A Roman flogging was a brutal form of punishment. Jesus would have been hit with thirty-nine or

223

more lashes of a whip made of braided leather thongs with metal balls and pieces of sharp bone woven into them. Each hit would have caused massive damage to His flesh, and He would have lost tons of blood."

He said, "How do you know that?"

I said, "I study, Dad. I look into history. Jesus was not the only guy who was flogged and crucified. Historians look into this stuff, and it is well documented. In fact, I made a note in my Bible right here. Listen, a third-century historian by the name of Eusebius described a flogging as: "For they say that the bystanders were struck with amazement when they saw them lacerated with scourges even to the innermost veins and arteries, so that the hidden inward parts of the body, both their bowels and their members, were exposed to view" (*Ecclesiastical History, Book 4, chap. 15*). A flogging really was brutal."

He said, "Yeah, sounds like it."

I said, "Yeah, but then it got worse. After that, He had to walk to the crucifixion point. Then He was nailed with a spike that was five to seven inches long tapered to a sharp point through his wrists or hands. The word *excruciating* was invented because there were no words to describe the pain, which literally means 'out of the cross.'

He said, "Is that true?"

I said, "As far as I have read, yes it is. Then spikes would have been driven through His feet. At this point His arms would have been stretched about six inches in length, and both shoulders would most likely have been dislocated. He would have had a lot of trouble breathing. Inhaling and exhaling would have eventually taken its toll on Him, and He probably died of cardiac arrest. Doctors have said that hypovolemic shock would have caused a sustained rapid heart rate that would have contributed to heart failure, resulting in the collection of fluid in the membrane around the heart, called pericardial effusion, as well as around the lungs, which is called pleural effusion."

He said, "What are you a doctor now?"

I said, "No, I am just reporting what I read on this subject. If you think about it, John, an eyewitness, saw blood and water come out after Jesus was crucified, which means the soldier pierced His heart, showing that His lungs had collapsed and He had died of asphyxiation. The Bible even reports this."

I then turned to John 19:34 and read out loud: "'Instead, one of the soldiers pierced Jesus' side with a spear, bringing a sudden flow of blood and water.' Ya see, when the soldier pierced his side, the spear apparently went through the right lung and into the heart, so when the spear was pulled out, some fluid came out. This would have had the appearance of a clear fluid, like water, followed by a large volume of blood, as the eyewitness John described. This was not a pleasant way to die, and to say that Jesus lived through it truly is an outrageous claim, as you can see."

He said, "Yeah, I guess Jesus making it through this would be highly unlikely."

I said, "Yeah, but there is more. Think about this. The Bible records that before He was buried, Jesus's body was prepared in the Jewish custom with spices and wrapped with linen. This process could possibly have weighed over one hundred pounds. So after the flogging and being crucified, Jesus then unwrapped Himself, neatly folded up the linen and put it by where He had been laying, rolled the stone away, snuck past the guards, and then the post resurrection appearances of Jesus are what convinced the disciples that Jesus defeated death? Don't you think it would be impossible for the disciples to have been so transformed and confident if Jesus had lived through this? He would have looked like a half-dead zombie. It just does not add up."

He said, "Okay, so maybe He was dead. But I am sure there is also an argument against every argument that you have made.."

I said, "You are one hundred percent correct. Have you heard them and decided for yourself which argument is most persuasive? These are not my arguments; some have been around for centuries. There are also other naturalistic theories that try to do everything in their power to stay away from a supernatural explanation. You have conspiracy theories, hallucination theories, myth theories, impersonation theories, spiritual resurrection theories, and the infamous unknown or wrong tomb theory. Each and every one of them can be debunked rather quickly. Are you interested in hearing them?"

He said, "No, I am good for now. I just don't understand what all of this has to do with me. I mean, so what? I am dying. I have no more hope! Doctors threw in the towel, and I am basically done. They might as well just throw me out on the sidewalk and let me die."

I said, "Dad, stop it. You have a new kind of hope to look toward now, and this has everything to do with you. You need to decide for yourself who Jesus really is. If He rose from the grave, which I believe He did, this means His power is available to you too. You never thought about things like this before, and there is no time like the present. Please think about it. I love you, and God loves you too. You should probably turn in for the night. I'll be right here."

He said, "I will give it some serious thought. I love you, son. Good night."

He fell asleep rather quickly, and I sat in that chair feeling pretty good about our conversation. I just prayed that he got something out of it and looked forward to some more conversations very soon.

He had some visitors that were in and out all the next day—my sisters and their kids, even his close friends and his ex-wife, my mother, came. He was really out of it, and it pained us all to see him like that.

I decided to stay the last night with him again, and the nurse in charge that night was a Christian. She was wonderful, full of faith, and even evangelized a little bit, but my dad kept saying, "Show me the proof!"

What was amazing is that she said, "Okay."

It turned out that she was a Roman Catholic and had just gotten back from a trip to Israel. She asked God to give her a sign while she was there, and she was heavily into the devotion of Mary, the mother of Jesus.

While I had my reservations about it, I kept quiet as she spoke. When she asked for a sign, she looked up into the clouds and saw a cloud formation that resembled a woman's face. She took a picture of it and showed it to my dad. I took a look at it as well, and I did have to admit that the cloud formation did resemble a woman's face. Whether it was Mary or not I truly do not know, and whether it was a sign or not is a matter of speculation, but it deeply confirmed her faith in God.

As amazing as it was, my dad was still not convinced, but I do believe it was worth a try, and I thanked her for sharing. She said to me that I was going to have my hands full with my dad, and I said, "No doubt, but please keep him in your prayers."

After she left the room, I said, "You know, Dad, whether the nurse showed you the picture or not, you sure could tell that she loved Jesus, how much her life was changed by being a Christian, and how much she wanted you to have this joy too, couldn't you?

He said, "Yeah, but I think the picture was a hoax."

I said, "I really don't think we can count it out. I think that all miracles should be tested on a case by case basis. I'll never know whether that was a true one or not, but it sure confirmed her faith in God. This is not the only miracle I had heard about concerning something with Mary. I read of a story that happened in nineteen eighty-one in a small village in Bosnia. Supposedly, six kids witnessed Mary appear to them on a mountain not just once but several times."

He said, "Really?"

I said, "Yeah, so I have read. It has attracted many people from all over the world, and it is known as the village of miracles now. There are shrines built everywhere, and these kids, who are not kids anymore, still see visions, and people just flock to them hoping for their own miracles."

He said, "What do you think about it?"

I said, "Honestly, I don't know what to think; I never really looked into it. I do know one thing though; I don't like to see Christians devoting so much time to Mary. Some even go as so far to worship her and even Roman Catholicism teaches differently. They want you to ask her to pray for you, not pray to her. It is grossly misinterpreted, and it takes devotion away from Jesus, which is just my opinion, of course."

He said, "This Jesus, you know I have been thinking about it, maybe He was just like a myth or something."

I said, "Dad, a myth can have a variety of meanings. It's an idea that develops into a story that is believed by many people that just is not true. There are not too many scholars out there who think Jesus was not a real person. And the scholars that do think that He did not exist really are not taken too seriously anymore. I actually know of just one, and everything that brings him to this conclusion is seriously just very strange. In all honesty, Jesus is mentioned outside of biblical sources that are very early. Christian sources, Jewish, non-Jewish, and Roman historians mention His name, sometimes His close followers, and even His brother James. It just is not reasonable to believe that He did not exist and was just a myth."

He said, "Okay, well, maybe He did exist, but His miracles and resurrection were just made up and developed over time."

I said, "Oh. Like Santa?"

He said, "Santa?"

I said, "Yeah, sure, think about it. There was a real guy who lived in the fourth century who was a Christian bishop in Turkey. He was known as St. Nicholas of Myra. He was known to give gifts to the poor. He even had a reputation as a secret gift giver and put coins in the shoes of people who left them outside. It is even said that he tossed coins through a window, and if the windows were locked, then he would drop the coins down the chimney. It is said that he was known to be bearded and also wore the color red and even a red hat. Then as time marched on, more stories were added to this real individual that are not true. Some are based on other myths. In the pre-Christian Norse tradition, Odin would often enter through chimneys, and in the Italian

Befana tradition, the gift-giving witch is covered with soot from her trips down the chimney."

He said, "How do you know all this?"

I said, "I like to read, Dad. I find this stuff very interesting. So the Santa Claus, St. Nick, Kris Kringle, or the jolly happy elf that we have come to know and kids love today, is based on an actual person, but as time went on, myths developed, and all of it certainly is not true. Now he lives in the North Pole, has reindeer, a magical sled, a work shop where his elves are employed, and goes around the world, hits every house, gives kids gifts underneath a tree, goes up and down the chimney, and so on. This is what you think happened with the Jesus story?"

He said, "Well, why not?"

I said, "Because it takes time for a story handed down through history to develop like that. There just was no time for anything like that to happen to the Jesus story. The story was based on eyewitness accounts or secondhand testimony that was reliable, and it was too early for legendary development.

He said, "How so?"

I said, "Well, in the New Testament, Jesus's closest disciple Peter discredits that notion of a myth or fable when he says°…"I then grabbed my Bible, turned to 2 Peter, and skimmed through it quickly. "Here it is. Let me read it to you. 'For we have not followed cunningly devised fables, when we made known unto you the power and coming of our Lord Jesus Christ, but were eyewitnesses of his majesty." (2 Peter 1:16) Plus there just was not enough time for a myth to develop. Usually, several generations have to pass before added mythological elements can be mistakenly believed to be facts. Eyewitnesses would have been around before that to discredit any new, mythic versions."

He said, "Sounds good, but I'm not convinced."

I said, "Well, let's look at the earliest writings in the New Testament that predate the Gospels—Matthew, Mark, Luke, and John. Let's go earlier to a letter from Paul. Most scholars agree that Paul's letters were written within the lifetime of the eyewitnesses of Jesus. If these letters are not myth, then the Gospels are not either, for Paul affirms all the main claims of the Gospels. But for argument's sake, let's look at the early creed from one Corinthians fifteen. Not just biblical scholars, but secular as well, date this as being written two to five years after Jesus's crucifixion. That's pretty early, right?"

He said, "Yeah, I guess."

I said, "Well, let me grab my Bible, and I'll read it to you."

He said, "Is it long?"

I said, "No. Okay, it says in one Corinthians, "'For I delivered unto you first of all that which I also received, how that Christ died for our sins according to the scriptures; And that he was buried, and that he rose again the third day according to the scriptures: And that he was seen of Cephas, then of the twelve: After that, he was seen of above five hundred brethren at once; of whom the greater part remain unto this present, but some are fallen asleep. After that, he was seen of James; then of all the apostles. And last of all he was seen of me also, as of one born out of due time.' (1 Corinthians 15:3-8) What do you think of that?"

He said, "I don't know what to think."

I said, "Well, think about this. Paul begins by saying, 'For I delivered unto you first of all that which I also received.' What is most important here is 'For I delivered unto you' and 'all that which I also received.' What this indicates is that Paul is giving the tradition he received and is passing on. This is known as a very early creed."

He said, "So what?"

I said, "I figured you would say that, but I'm not done. What you probably don't know is that Paul did not walk with Jesus while Jesus had His earthly ministry. As a matter of fact, Paul persecuted Christians after Jesus's crucifixion. He was very against Christianity until he had his conversion on Damascus road. Let me read to you his conversion from Acts. 'And Saul, yet breathing out threatenings and slaughter against the disciples of the Lord, went unto the high priest, And desired of him letters to Damascus to the synagogues, that if he found any of this way, whether they were men or women, he might bring them bound unto Jerusalem. And as he journeyed, he came near Damascus: and suddenly there shined round about him a light from heaven: And he fell to the earth, and heard a voice saying unto him, Saul, Saul, why persecutest thou me? And he said, Who art thou, Lord? And the Lord said, I am Jesus whom thou persecutest: it is hard for thee to kick against the pricks. And he trembling and astonished said, Lord, what wilt thou have me to do? And the Lord said unto him, Arise, and go into the city, and it shall be told thee what thou must do. And the men which journeyed with him stood speechless, hearing a voice, but seeing no man. And Saul arose from the earth; and when his eyes were opened, he saw no man: but they led him by the hand, and brought him into Damascus. And he was three days without sight, and neither did eat nor drink'" (Acts 9:1–9).

He said, "I really don't want a Bible study."

I said, "Okay, but that was important for you to understand because Paul then was baptized, received his sight back, and became very vocal for Christianity. His conversion can be dated probably within five years after Jesus's crucifixion. He received the early creed that I read to you at his conversion when he met other Christians or maybe three years later when he visited Peter and James in Jerusalem. The point is that in the creed Paul states that He was buried and that He rose again the third day according to the scriptures: 'And that he was seen of Cephas (who is Peter), then of the twelve: After that, he was seen of above five hundred brethren at once; of whom the greater part remain unto this present, but some are fallen asleep. After that, he was seen of James; then of all the apostles. And last of all he was seen of me also, as of one born out of due time.' Jesus was seen by many people after His death, and the only explanation is that God raised Him from the dead. These are eyewitnesses, and in a sense Paul was saying, 'If you don't believe me, go check with the people who saw him, some of them are still alive.' Isn't that amazing, Dad? Being a DEA agent, you can understand the importance of eyewitness testimony, right?"

He said, "Yeah, I guess."

I said, "Listen, we have been up for quite a while talking. Why don't you meditate on our conversation a little bit and then get some sleep."

We called the nurse in to put the BIPAP mask on him, and he fell asleep. I prayed all night that what we had been talking about would sink in. We would be leaving at some point the following day to take him to the rehab place at the nursing home. I knew it was going to be a big day, and I just could not wait to get out of the hospital room we were in. I wondered what tomorrow would bring. Whatever it did bring, I was thankful to have another day with my dad.

CHAPTER 13

Transport

The next day a lot of people came to see him, mostly close family and friends. I had not been home in a couple of days, and my daughter was having a graduation ceremony (kindergarten to first grade) later on in the day. I decided I was going to go home, take a much-needed shower, change my clothes, and go see her and my wife at the school. The nursing home was going to send a transport van to pick up my dad and bring him to the nursing home later on in the afternoon or early evening. I was very excited to have him a lot closer to home. The hospital he was in was forty-five minutes away, and the nursing home would be about a twenty-five minute drive.

I got into my car, and it was a very hot and humid day. I'll never forget how much sweat beaded off of my temples as soon as I got in my car. The weatherman on the radio said it was the hottest day of the summer, and I sure could see why.

I got home and did what I needed to do. I even had time to take a quick nap in my own bed and then I was off to my daughter's school. The ceremony was going to be outside, and when I tell you it was a hot day, it sure was; I could not believe they were not having it inside in the air-conditioning to keep everyone cool.

My wife and I were standing outside waiting for the kids to come out along with all of the other parents, and I was just miserable. I could not get my dad out of my mind. I was really upset, and the humidity was not making the situation any better. I spent a little time with my wife and daughter before the ceremony, but I just could not be out in that hot sun any longer with my mind racing about my dad.

I told my wife to forgive me, but I just had to go back to the hospital. She understood, and I walked to my car. I got in my car and immediately I began to sweat again when I sat on the driver's seat. I turned the air conditioner on, which blew out hot air before the car warmed up.

I thought to myself, *I am just miserable. God, give me strength.*

I started to drive and then came to an intersection where I could only make a left or a right. The light was green, so I put my left turn signal on and started to make my turn. Out of corner of my eye I saw a young man on a motorcycle with no helmet, wearing a shirt with cut-off sleeves and jeans, going at least thirty miles per hour coming straight toward me on my left.

I don't know what he was thinking; I clearly had a green light. It all happened so fast! He hit his brakes, I hit mine, and I tried to swerve out of the way to avoid him. His motorcycle now was about to hit my driver's side back wheel area!

He skidded off of the bike, the bike hit my car, and as my car came to a stop. I then watched in horror as he tumbled and scraped his body on the concrete road.

My heart was pounding, my adrenaline was rushing, and I thought that he was dead. I got out of my car as fast as I could and ran over to him, which was about thirty feet away.

He was lying on his back, there was noticeable blood running down his knees, elbows, and scrapes all over arms.

As I ran over to him, I said, "Are you all right? Let me call the police."

He got to his feet and walked over to his motorcycle, which had obvious damage. He checked it out and said, "I am okay. Please don't call the police. What were you doing? I had a green light!"

I said, "Really? I know that I had a green light, bud, but seriously, we have to call the police and get an ambulance here."

He said, "Please don't. I don't have a license."

I said, "Are you serious? And you are not even wearing a helmet? You are limping, man; we have to get you to a hospital."

He tried to start his motorcycle, but it would not start. He pushed it off the road and said, "I'm fine. Let's just forget about this. I don't want to get in trouble."

I said, "Look, man, I don't know about this."

I then looked over at my car and noticed that my driver's side rear tire was flat and had a gaping hole in it. I knew that something sharp on his bike gashed it at the point of impact.

He started walking away with his bike down the street. I walked toward my car to assess the damage, and all of a sudden an undercover cop comes flying down the road. He got out of his car and ran over to the guy.

Next thing I know there were two more cop cars and an ambulance there. They were all on the other side of the street about three hundred feet away from me.

I was just glad the ambulance was there, but I was not sure what this guy was telling everyone. If he did not have a license, things could get really ugly. I did not know what to do. I had just gotten into an accident, a motorcyclist almost got killed, my dad was in the hospital dying, the police were everywhere, and now I had to change my tire in this blistering, hot, and humid heat.

Talk about miserable.

I changed my tire, and a police officer finally came over to talk to me. I looked like I had just jumped into a pool from all the sweat that was coming off of me.

It turned out that the first police officer that came onto the scene had witnessed the entire accident. He knew who was at fault, and I did not get a ticket. The guy on the motorcycle was actually wanted and was in a gang. The police officer said that if I needed a report of the accident for insurance purposes to let him know.

I said, "Thanks, but no thanks. The only damage I have is a flat tire. It's not the end of the world, and I am just happy that the guy is okay. He apparently has enough problems, and I don't need any more problems. I got enough going on."

I then was on my way. I headed to the first gas station that I saw and bought a much-needed Gatorade. I thought to myself, *What a day. Now I'm off to the hospital to see my dad and wait for the transport van to pick him up. This is one day that is going down in the books as unforgettable. God, I really need some strength to get through this day, and it is only two o'clock in the afternoon!*

I got to the hospital, and my two younger sisters were there. I told them what had happened because I looked like I was in a train wreck from all of the sweat. They told me that my one sister had gotten into a heated argument with the nurse who was taking care of my dad. She had apparently crossed the line by telling her that their kids had to leave, there were too many people in the room, it was too loud, and she had given some unprofessional parenting advice. Everyone was clearly upset, the kids were home, and now the head social worker was on her way into the room to talk to my sister about what had happened.

We waited in the hospital room all afternoon with my dad. It was a long day, and all my dad kept talking about was having a cigarette. He said he would only cooperate if he could get one, and we diffused the situation by telling him once we got him outside, we would get him one.

After an emotionally draining day, finally the transport driver walked into his room with a wheelchair around seven thirty. We were glad to go, but my dad said he would not leave or get into the van until he had a cigarette.

My dad was hooked up to an oxygen tank, and a tube was in his nose. The transport driver said that he could not allow him to have a cigarette. My dad looked over at me, and I'll never forget the look on his face, because he looked so helpless, and he said very sadly, "Billy, you promised."

I said, "Dad, I promise you that you will have a cigarette before you walk through the doors in the nursing home. Just please cooperate."

He said, "Good enough for me."

My two sisters and I all got into our separate cars and followed the transport van, but I needed to stop by an ATM machine, buy a pack of cigarettes for him, and withdraw some money because my plan was to talk to the transport driver, slip him some money, unhook my dad's oxygen, and let him have a smoke before he took him in to his room.

I pulled into the nursing home parking lot and there was the van parked out front by the doors to get in. My sisters were standing there with the transport driver, my dad in his wheelchair, the oxygen tank unhooked, and my dad was finally having a smoke.

It turned out that my dad was able to have a conversation with the driver on the way there, my little sister had a pack of cigarettes on her, and they talked him into letting him have a smoke.

After the whole ordeal, he only took about six puffs and put it out. I gave the transport driver a couple of bucks and said, "Thank you."

We settled my dad into his new room, his new nurses and aides then took over, and he went to sleep rather quickly. We all left and went home to get a much-needed night of sleep. This happened on a Friday, and I had taken so much time off of work. I thanked God that my boss was so understanding, but I had to get back to work that Monday. My dad was going to start physical therapy that Monday and he was going to have a busy schedule.

The nursing home was very accommodating, and the next day I was able to bring my dad's dog to see him. I have never seen him so happy before in my life. It was the first time I had seen him smile since he got this life-changing news. Ralph jumped onto his bed, licked him, and my dad pet him like he had never pet him before. These two were made for each other, and if a dog could smile, Ralph sure was smiling when he saw my dad.

I thought to myself, *When my dad adopted and saved this dog, who really saved who?* It truly was a beautiful moment, and I just knew that I had to bring Ralph to see Dad as much as possible.

Friends and family were in and out all day visiting him. My wife and kids were even able to come for a little while. They had not had much of a chance to see him while he was in the hospital. He seemed to be in better spirits now than when he was in the hospital, which was good to see, but then he began to act like his old self and told a nurse that she had a nice rear end.

When I tell you that my dad said things that were on his mind, this is the kind of thing I was talking about. We told him that he could not say things like that, but telling him he couldn't do something just made him angry. He did not understand why he could not say that. He said that he was just giving her a compliment! That was my dad. You either loved the guy or you could not stand him!

The next day was Sunday, and I had a lot to do at home, so I came in the evening to see my dad, and no one was there visiting with him. I brought Ralph again, and he jumped into bed with him. Dad was happy to see him, but there was an obvious change in his behavior, and he seemed really down in the dumps. I asked him, "What's wrong, Dad? Do you not like it here?"

He said, "I want to go home. I want to smoke. I want to go to the casino. I want to do things again that I want to do. I can't do anything anymore."

I said, "Dad, you are here to try and rehabilitate yourself. You are going to try to do physical therapy to get your legs moving again. You have been restricted to a bed for a long time. They have to try to get you moving around. You have to listen and do what these people tell you to do. They are only trying to help."

He said, "Then can I come home? I don't want to be alone anymore."

My heart was breaking for him. What a total role reversal this was for me; telling my dad when and if he can come home.

I said, "If you want to come home, then we will figure a way out to do that. In the meantime, just please try to do this therapy, okay?"

He said, "I miss my house. I miss my dog. I don't want to die, but if and when I do, I want to die at home. I don't want to be alone anymore."

I said, "Dad, I know you miss being at home. I never in my wildest dreams would have thought that when we left the house to go to the emergency room with your legs swollen it would come to this. I know you are scared, I know that you hate to be alone, but you don't have to be scared and you don't have to be alone anymore. God loves you so much, and He is just waiting for you. Stop being so stubborn and hard-hearted and just let Him in. He has so many wonderful promises. He can help you cast off your fears and the feeling of being alone. He will never leave you or forsake you. He says not to fear, for He is with you. He says that He will strengthen you. He says that He will help you. He says not to be afraid, you are worth more than many sparrows."

He said, "I am just so scared to die and be alone."

I said, "You don't have to be. Just listen to me, Dad. There is nothing to fear when you let God in. You do not have to die alone. I remember you once told me that you had a favorite scripture. You probably don't remember what it is, do you?"

He said, "Yeah. I remember. It is the one with the staff."

I said, "Yes! You are right."

I reached into my bag, pulled out my Bible, and turned to Psalm 23.

I said, "Dad, please close your eyes, listen to these words, and let them soak in."

I looked at him, and he closed his eyes very slowly. I couldn't believe it! He was actually listening to me!

I said, "'The LORD is my shepherd; I shall not want. He maketh me to lie down in green pastures: he leadeth me beside the still waters. He restoreth my soul: he leadeth me in the paths of righteousness for his name's sake. Yea, though I walk through the valley of the shadow of death, I will fear no evil: for thou art with me; thy rod and thy staff they comfort me. Thou preparest a table before me in the presence of mine enemies: thou anointest my head with oil; my cup runneth over. Surely goodness and mercy shall follow me all the days of my life: and I will dwell in the house of the LORD for ever.'"

Dad, God can and will, if you let Him in, restore your soul. Though you walk through the valley of the shadow of death, you do not have to fear evil for God can be with you; His rod and His staff can comfort you. You can dwell in the house of the LORD forever. This is eternal life, Dad. All you have to do is believe this. The most awesome part about it is that no one can just say they believe this on their own. Jesus said, 'No man can come to me, except the Father which hath sent me draw him: and I will raise him up at the last day.' I forget what the Greek word is for *draw*, plus I would not know how to say it anyway. But these words were originally written in Greek. As a matter of fact, the entire New Testament was. But I do know that in the Greek language *draw* means "to drag." God does the drawing or dragging, but we who are drawn have a responsibility to respond. He is not going to drag you kicking and screaming if you do not want to come to Him. But in all honestly, I am going to tell you right now, if you believe this with a true heart and let God in, He will change you from the inside out, and you will have an overwhelming sense of peace that transcends anything that you can possibly describe or fathom. It is a feeling that only a true Christian can explain. Only God can do this. I have it, as do many others, and there were many before us who did too and died in peace. They are now reaping the benefits of trusting God. All you have to do is believe this, Dad. Do you? Can you?"

He opened his eyes, was very quiet for about thirty seconds while he stared into space. He finally said, "It is easier said than done, Billy. I am going to die for, Christ's sake."

I said, "Dad, I realize that, but someday I will be in your position. We all will—my wife, my kids, your kids, and death can happen at any time. I might just get into a car accident on my way home from here and die behind the wheel, you never know. But I take great comfort in knowing that this life is not all there is. Pain, suffering, death, sickness, and all the evil in the world—there just *has* to be more than this. I have felt His presence, seen too much, experienced too much, and all the evidence points to Jesus's Resurrection being true. When we put our trust in Christ, the One who conquered death, we are promised an eternal home with Him where there is no more pain and suffering, only joy. I want this for you, and more importantly, so does God. He is not going to make you though. It is up to you. The choice is yours."

He said, "I can tell how strongly you believe this. But we just don't know if it is true. Plus, there is nothing that can stop you from believing this."

I said, "No, Dad. This is where you are wrong. Though it would break my heart to come to find out that my faith is not real, but I would walk away from Christianity if it were found to be false."

He said, "What do you mean?"

I said, "Like I said, if the resurrection of Jesus was proven false somehow, I would walk away."

He said, "Really?"

I said, "Yes. I would have to look for alternative explanations for everything that I have experienced in my walk with Christ, and I do believe that this would be very difficult to do. It would totally destroy the Christian faith, and there is no way around it. It would prove that Jesus and the early disciples were liars, deceived the world, and it was the biggest conspiracy ever set forth in history, but you know what the problem is with that?"

He said, "What?"

I said, "This would not explain the disciples, eyewitnesses, and early Christians willingly persecuted, martyred, and dying for a lie. This just does not make sense. People will die for their faith in any religion because they believe it to be true, but to know what you actually believe is a lie and then to willing die just does not add up. Anyway, think about it. I have to get going, because I have to go to work tomorrow. I love you. I'll stop by after work tomorrow, but I don't get out until six thirty. I'll come directly here, so I won't be bringing Ralph tomorrow, but I'll bring him to see you soon. Give what we talked about some thought, and I'll be praying for you. I love you."

He said, "Thanks, Billy. I love you too."

I let him say his good-byes to Ralph, I kissed him on his forehead, and left. I felt that we'd had a very productive conversation, and I prayed the whole way home.

It felt good to be back at work. My boss had been very understanding with me leaving early, coming in late, and taking full days off to be with my dad. We were very busy most of the day, but I could not get my dad off of my mind. For some reason I could not get out of my head how much he loved playing slots at the casino. I felt led to write down some special statistics about probability and chance since my dad just loved being around this stuff. I would bring it along with me, and we could talk about it when I went to see him that night after work.

After work, I drove straight to the nursing home and made it there in about an hour and fifteen minutes. When I pulled into the parking lot, I grabbed my bag with my Bible in it and the special notes I had written down about probability and chance that I was going to share with him.

I walked into the building, and the older residents were all gathered around a couch talking. One woman stopped me and asked where my dog was. I told her that Ralph was at home, but I would make sure to bring him by this weekend. They really loved that dog! He put a smile on everyone's faces!

As I walked around the corner to my dad's room, I heard someone talking. I peeked in to see who it was, and there sitting in a chair next to my dad's bed was a good friend of my mother. She was such a beautiful person, had a loving spirit about her, and she was a Christian.

I decided not to go in and eavesdrop a little bit to see what they were talking about. So I stood there for a good twenty minutes while I listened to her tell my dad about Jesus and how much God loved him. She was so loving in the way that she presented the gospel. She even gave him a special small Bible that only had the New Testament and Psalms. As a fellow Christian, I appreciated what she was trying to do, but he just was so put off by everything she was saying. He kept saying, "Give me proof; give me proof!"

I could empathize with what she was going through. She had a lot of patience, and you could sense how much she cared about him. Unfortunately, he just was not open to the message and certainly was not responsive. She finally said to him that she had to leave, but it was nice seeing him, and to think about what she said.

When she walked out of the room I was standing there, and I told her that I was listening in on the conversation. I thanked her for taking the time out of her day to come see him and more importantly to share the gospel with him. I also told her not to take offense to him being so stubborn and that I went through it all the time. I told her that her words had not fallen on deaf ears—she was watering the seeds that I and others had planted, but it was up to God to make them grow. I told her to have a good evening and keep him in her prayers. I also asked her to keep me in her prayers as I was going to continue ministering to him and that I could use all the prayers I could get. It would take a miracle for my dad to respond to the gospel.

She thanked me, walked away, and then I entered the room and sat down in the same chair that she sat in.

He was watching television, and I said, "Hey, Dad, how are you doing?"

He said, "Ahh. All right I guess. One of yoose was just here."

I said, "One of yoose? What do you mean?"

He said, "You know, one of you Bible people. Your mother's friend came and told me about Jesus. She even gave me that book sitting on the table."

I grabbed the book, skimmed through it, and said, "You would enjoy this. You should take the time to read it."

He said, "I would, but I'm a busy guy. I don't have the time."

I said, "Yeah, I guess you're right. You know, Dad, she took the time out of her busy day just to come up here and see you. I think you could be a little grateful for that, don't you think?"

He said, "She just wanted to preach to me."

I said, "And what does she gain by that? She is not being compensated or making money for doing it. She is just showing her Christian love for you by sharing the message that God loves you. Is that so wrong?"

He said, "I guess not."

I said, "People who do that only do it because they care. How did your rehab go today?"

He said, "I hated it. They want me to walk and then stand in a circle with all the old people and roll a beach ball back and forth to one another. I feel like I am in a mental hospital just for old people. People sit around in their wheelchairs staring at the wall, and they play these stupid games and do puzzles. This is just so dumb. I do not see any point in this. I just want to go home."

I said, "I'm sure there is a point to it all, Dad. Listen, have you thought about our conversation from last night?"

He said, "Yeah. I thought about it, and I just need proof."

I said, "You and your proof that you require! You are unbelievable. I don't know what kind of proof you are looking for that would convince you. I am getting to the point where I believe you are so biased in your thinking that there is no way to convince you. It is impossible to persuade someone to believe something else if his or her mind is already made up."

He said, "Then show me proof, and I'll believe what you are saying."

I said, "I really feel like we are just going around in circles here. You are scared and feel alone, I am offering you a solution to your problem, and you just do not want it. Listen, I want to tell you a quick story. Have you ever heard of a guy by the name of Charles Spurgeon?"

He said, "I think so, but what about him?"

I said, "Well, he was a famous preacher in England from the eighteen hundreds. He was known as the Prince of Preachers and was highly admired. His work still to this day influences many Christians. Anyway, since you desire proof, I think that this might help. He once said, 'I heard the story of a man, a blasphemer, profane, an atheist, who was converted singularly by a sinful action of his.' Do you think that is possible for an atheist to do that, Dad? Going from a life of believing that God does not exist to believing that He does?"

He said, "I don't know. It would have to be some pretty hefty proof. What happened?"

I said, "Well, this atheist had written on a piece of paper°…" At this point, I took a piece of paper, placed it on the table in front of my dad, and wrote "God is nowhere."

I said, "The atheist wrote 'God is nowhere.' He then ordered his child to read it because he thought that it would make him an atheist too."

He said, "I'm not sure how that could make his child be an atheist."

I said, "Well, you will see that it did not, and his plan backfired. What happened was the atheist made the child write down on a piece of paper the same exact thing. He told him to write 'God is nowhere.' The child picked up the pen, and I am sure he was very nervous and frightened, and wrote°…"

At this point I wrote down on the same paper "God is now here."

I said, "The child spelled it, "God is *now* here." You see, Dad, it was a truth instead of a lie, and the arrow pierced the man's own heart. And as the story goes, at that very moment the atheist became a believer in God and a Christian. God worked through this child to show this atheist that He does exist. God uses and works through people and circumstances all the time. All of these proofs that you are looking for are right in front of you. People are persuaded to think differently in many amazing ways. You just need to open your eyes."

He said, "Well, that is a pretty amazing story, but can we prove that it is true?"

I said, "Here we go again. I think that even if this pen began to write on a piece of paper all by itself, and the words came on to the paper "Here is your proof," you still would not believe because your mind is already made up."

He said, "Not true."

I said, "Dad, the evidence is all around you. Just open your eyes and heart to the possibility. I know you love the casino, and I want to talk about it a little. I really feel led to share with you from the standpoint of mathematics and probability, also known as odds, which is a branch of mathematics that measures the likelihood that a given event will occur. I am about to share with you some amazing odds. Are you up for listening?"

He said, "If we are going to talk about the casino, then I am all ears. I cannot wait to go back!"

I said, "I'll get to that, but first I want to share with you some probabilities that mathematicians have figured out. This is not my math, so you can be assured that it is not wrong."

I grabbed my notes and said: "The odds of being struck by lightning in a year is 7×10^5 or 1 in 700,000. The odds of being killed by lightning in a year is 2×10^6 or 1 in 2,000,000. The odds of becoming president is 1×10^7 or 1 in 10,000,000. The odds of a meteorite landing on your house is 1.8×10^{14} or 1 in 180,000,000,000,000. If you are having a hard time with these figures, like I am, I'll give you an easy one. The odds that you will eventually die is 1 in 1. Do you think you can agree so far?"

He said, "Well, I guess so. Those are some crazy odds."

I said, "Yes, they are. Okay, let's talk about the casino now. I know that you are all too familiar with playing the slot machines. So what do you think the odds are for you to pull the handle and get the jackpot?"

He said, "Not very good."

I said, "Yes, I agree, but you keep trying, don't ya?"

He said, "Yeah, because you never know."

I said, "Sure. But the odds of hitting the jackpot on a three-wheel slot machine are eight million to one! I think you play the five wheel, so you can only imagine the odds of winning the jackpot on that. Obviously it is higher than eight million to one. Maybe it is double, I don't know. Let's just say now it is twenty-four million to one. The odds of you hitting it are really not that good, now are they? You would have to agree that the odds of you winning are pretty much slim to none."

He said, "Well, when you put it that way, I guess so."

I said, "I now want to talk to you about Bible prophecy, which in a way talks about probability and chance."

He said, "Great. Only you could figure out a way to talk about Jesus and the casino."

I said, "I can sense the sarcasm, but just stay with me, because I know that you will find this interesting. Think of Jesus like a slot machine."

He said, "How?"

I said, "You will see. What you must first understand is that the writings in the Old Testament were written possibly five hundred to more than sixteen hundred years before Jesus was even born. Are you following me?"

He said, "Yeah. It's not that complicated."

I said, "Okay. Now, what I am going to talk about is a certain prophecy with predictions about Jesus in the Old Testament, which as you can see was written centuries before He was born, and how He fulfilled them. The fact of matter is that these prophecies were either written down by divine inspiration, or they were just lucky. Do you want to hear some stats?"

He said, "Sure. Go ahead."

I said, "These are not my calculations, they were done by mathematicians. So the probability of just one man fulfilling eight prophecies, multiplying eight probabilities together, gives us 2.8×10^{28}, or for simplicity sake 1×10^{28} or 1 in 10,000,000,000,000,000,000,000,000,000. Are you following?"

He said, "No, not really. That is a pretty big number."

I said, "I agree. It gets bigger though, because the chance that any one man fulfilled forty-eight prophecies to be 1 in 10 to the power of 157, or 1 in 10,00,000,000,000,000,00 0,000,000,000,000,000,000,000,000,000,000,000,0 00,000,000,000,000,000,000,000,000,000,000,000,000, 000,000,000,000,000,000,000,000,000,000,000,000,00

0,000,000,000,000,000 000,000,000. What do you think of that?"

He said, "This number is for forty-eight prophecies? Is this where you are going to tell me that Jesus fulfilled like fifty?"

I said, "Nope. Here are a couple of pieces of paper that I printed out for you. It lists three hundred and fifty-four prophecies in the Old Testament about Jesus fulfilling them in the New Testament. They are prophecies concerning His virgin birth, to the town He would be born in, to a detailed description of the crucifixion, which is remarkable because crucifixion wasn't even invented yet, to His side being pierced, and so on. Now three hundred and fifty-four might be kind of high, and I really did not look at this list thoroughly, but most biblical scholars would agree that Jesus fulfilled one hundred to one hundred and twenty of them. Pretty remarkable, isn't it, Dad?"

He said, "Yeah, but all this math was probably done by Christians."

I said, "Sure, but math doesn't lie. It doesn't matter if you are a Christian or not, two plus two will always be four. Jesus fulfilling these prophecies cannot be considered lucky. If you pulled the handle on a slot machine and hit the jackpot eight times in row, it is no longer luck. How about a hundred to a hundred and fifty times in a row? Dad, in all honesty, all jokes aside, do you believe in God?"

He said, "I really don't know what to believe anymore. I do believe that there is someone in charge up there."

I said, "Well, that is a start. If there is someone in charge up there, then there must be a heaven. What do you think it takes for someone to go to heaven?"

He said, "You know, like do good things."

I said, "So doing good things will get you to heaven? Do you consider yourself a good person?"

He said, "Yeah. I'm a pretty good guy. I have done some good stuff in my time."

I said, "Well, what about the bad things? I am sure you have done some bad things in your life too, right?"

He said, "Yeah, but the good things will cross out the bad things with God."

I said, "So this is what you are thinking God is like—when and if you stand before Him someday, He will have like a scale of some sort? Your good deeds will go on one side and your bad deeds will go on the other, and then your good deeds will outweigh the bad deeds, and then God will let you into heaven? I am just trying to visualize how you see this."

He said, "Yeah. Something like that."

I said, "This sounds like some sort of judgment. The Bible describes a judgment similar to this as well in the book of Hebrews: "And as it is appointed unto men once to die, but after this the judgment." (Heb. 9:27). But there is a *huge* difference between your view of judgment and the Bible's view of judgment. You know, a lot of people think like this. But there is a huge problem with this because you and all these people think that your good will outweigh the bad. Some people even think that God will overlook their bad. I am going to start using the word *sin* instead of the word *bad*. I don't think you quite grasp what the word *sin* really is, do you? What is sin?"

He said, "Bad things."

I said, "Sin goes deeper than that, Dad. Our sin is what keeps us from having a relationship with God. We live in a fairly amoral world that believes each person can decide what is right, what is true, and what is moral,-whatever that might mean. Television, movies, and the people we are supposed to look up to don't help with their portrayals of happy people blatantly living sinful lives. But the fact of the matter is that God has set standards about right and wrong, and there is such thing as sin. God is holy and perfect; people are sinful. We are all sinners, as Paul says in the book of Romans, 'For all have sinned, and come short of the glory of God' (Rom. 3:23). Sin can mean even not understanding or caring about what is right. We defy God when we know what is right and then refuse to do it. James tells us this "Anyone, then, who knows the good he ought to do and doesn't do it, sins" (James 4:17). Isaiah tells us that 'our iniquities have separated us from God' (Isaiah 59:2). Are you following me?"

He said, "Yeah."

I said, "Okay. So now that you have an understanding of how God views sin, tell me how when you stand before Him at this judgment with this scale you are talking about you will gain entry into heaven? Isaiah said, 'But we are all as an unclean thing, and all our righteousnesses (or good deeds) are as filthy rags; and we all do fade as a leaf; and our iniquities, like the wind, have taken us away (Isaiah 64:6). Your sin sits on one side, and your good deeds on the other just blow off the scale with a gust of wind like a bunch of leaves. Do you see what I am getting at?"

He said, "Yeah, I see what you are saying."

I said, "In all honesty, Dad, there is only one person who ever lived that walked this earth that is without sin. Peter says, 'Who did no sin, neither was guile found in His mouth' (1 Peter 2:22). This is Jesus. In two Corinthians it says, 'For he hath made him to be sin for us, who knew no sin; that we might be made the righteousness of God in him' (2 Cor.5:21). I know you don't want me spouting scripture, but you are looking for truth, and you need to look to Jesus. John says that Jesus answered, 'I am the way and the truth and the life. No one comes to the Father except through me'" (John 14:6).

He said, "So what does all of this mean?"

I said, "Jesus died to take the penalty for our sins that we deserved. In essence, He took our punishment so that we wouldn't have to. Jesus is the bridge that fills the gap to the way to God. He proved this with His life, death, and resurrection. Look, I know we have been talking about this for a while, and I don't want to lose you. Just give it some thought. How are they treating you here? How is the food?"

He said, "It is horrible. It is the same thing over and over again. I really want to come home."

I said, "Why? You are eating a lot better here. All you eat at home is the microwave meals, and they are not very good for you! At least here you are getting the proper nutrients."

He said, "I'll go out to eat and eat good food. A nice filet mignon with mashed potatoes. That would be great."

I said, "That does sound good. Listen, I have been here a while. I'm going to get going. Give what I said some thought, okay?"

He said, "Hang on a minute. I think I am ready."

I said, "What do you mean? What are you ready for?"

He said, "I think I am ready to become one of yoose now."

I said, "One of yoose? What are you talking about?"

He said, "You know. One of those guys who follow Jesus. What do I have to do? Sign something?"

My heart nearly stopped, and I thought I was going to have a stroke or a heart attack. Is this the moment I had been praying for so many years? Was my dad about to put his faith into Christ?

I said, "Are you serious? Because there is no turning back. Once God draws you and you respond, you are in His loving care from here on out, in this life and the next."

He said, "Yeah, now what do I sign, and what do I have to do?"

I said, "Dad, you don't have to sign anything or do anything; that is what is so amazing about God's love and His mercy. We are saved by grace just by putting our faith in Jesus. All you need to do is believe and trust what Jesus did for you by confessing out loud and believing in your heart that Jesus was raised form the dead. This is what the Bible says. Do you believe this?"

He said, "I do. I do now. So that's it?"

I said, "Yes, that is it. You believed in your heart and you confessed with your mouth, but you can also say a prayer to God. Ask Him to forgive you of your sins. I can't do it for you. That would be like you cheating on your wife and asking me to apologize to her for you."

I laughed a little bit.

He said, "Well, I really don't know how."

I said, "Well, while I was in the hospital with you last week, I wrote you out a prayer and said that when and if you were ready to do this to use the prayer or say something like it and believe it."

He said, "Where is it?"

I had it in my pocket, and I gave it to him. Then, on the evening of June 15, 2015, in Sellersville, Pennsylvania, in a rehabilitation room at Rockhill Mennonite Nursing Home, my dad swallowed his pride and humbled himself for the first time in his life and asked Jesus Christ to be his Lord and Savior. He looked over the piece of paper with the prayer that I had written, closed his eyes, and said, "God, this is the first time in my life I am going to really believe. I believe that You died and were resurrected, and You said that all who believe this will go to heaven. Lord, cleanse me of my sin, make me a new person. I thank you for dying for me. In Jesus's name, amen"

I felt an overwhelming peace at that point, and he said that he did too. I told him that he had made the most important decision of his life. I also told him that he did not have to fear death anymore because when he took his last breath, he can be assured that the next time he opened his eyes he would be with Jesus, and there is no other better place to be.

He then asked me for a pen. I gave him one, and he took the piece of paper that the prayers was on, signed his name at the bottom, and dated it. He said it was all official now and gave it to me. He said to give it to the "big guy."

I laughed a little and then took notice that he wrote down the wrong year. He wrote 2016! I asked him what year he thought it was, and he actually thought it was 2016! I told him that it was only 2015. I guess the time being away from home in the hospital and in the rehab really made him think that a year had flown by that quickly. We laughed for a little bit about that.

I left his room that night feeling really good. I could not believe that it had actually happened. On the way home, while I was driving, I just could not stop crying. Tears of joy streamed down my face. It was an amazing experience. God sure does answer prayers—it may take months, a year, a couple of years, or even many years, but He does answer prayers no matter how long it takes.

I told my wife as soon as I got home. She was in disbelief at first, as I am sure anyone who knew my dad as well as we did would be, but then she shared in my excitement.

The next morning, I sent my older sister who is Roman Catholic a message that simply said, "You are not going to believe what happened last night."

She responded, "I already know."

I responded, "What do you know?"

She responded, "I talked to Dad, and he said, 'Guess what? I'm one of yoose now.'"

His heavy New York accent was the icing on the cake.

Although I could be at peace knowing that his eternal salvation was secure, another chapter in all of our lives was about to begin. We had to come to terms that my dad was going to die, and it was not going to be an easy process for anyone, especially him.

CHAPTER 14

Hospice

The month of June was a very tough month for my dad while he tried to rehabilitate himself at the nursing home. All in all, he just could not make the effort to do physical therapy. I don't know whether it was because he was mentally or physically unable, or it may have been a combination of both. He was miserable, and he was not making any progress. After many meetings with the nurses we had come to find out that he was not working the system, therefore nothing more could help, plus his insurance would no longer pay 100 percent of the coverage, so we needed to look for alternatives.

Long story short, we all knew that he just wanted to come home, so now it was time to contact a hospice company. But there was also a huge dilemma because there would not be someone from hospice with him all the time. He needed to have someone with him twenty-four hours a day; there just was no way around it. He needed someone to cook for him, take him to the bathroom, make sure his oxygen machine was working correctly, and make sure he was taking his pills.

What he needed was a full-time aide as well as hospice to care for him.

My older sister who lived in Georgia had the summer off because she was a schoolteacher. She decided that she would move in with him for the summer and be his full-time aide. I do not think there are many people in the world that would do such a thing, considering how much work it was going to entail, but bless her heart, she did it for my dad.

She packed her things, took a flight, we picked her up at the Philadelphia airport on June 30, and she officially moved in. In the process, we called hospice and they came to set up everything in his apartment. A hospital bed, a toilet with handles, an oxygen machine, a BIPAB machine—you name it, it was there, and his apartment had everything he needed.

He now would be assigned a nurse who would come twice a week, a nurse's aide who would come every day, a chaplain who would come when needed, and a case manager/social worker.

I packed my dad's things at the nursing home, picked him up, and on July 1, we finally brought him home. He was very happy to be home, to say the least, but what we had to come to terms with was that he had come home to essentially die. When this was going to happen, nobody knew, but he was in his final stages of life.

It was hard to see at first. He was up and about, walking around, maybe a bit slower, but he still seemed to be his old self. A couple of different nurse's aides were sent out, and my dad finally hit it off with one of them. She was such a sweetheart. My brother-in-law stayed with my sister for a while, and they got him out and about and even to the casino.

It was a great last summer for him all in all. We had a Fourth of July picnic where lots of family and friends came. My dad had many visitors over the duration of the summer. Lots of close family, including my two sisters who lived in the area, as well as my mother (my dad's ex-wife—they formed a special bond through the experience) stopped by when they could, and even friends from all over the country came out to spend time with him. Some friends that he had not seen in many years from his high school days, Marine Corps days, the DEA, and his corporate work life. I know that he enjoyed that very much. He even had his fish guy and his ex-girlfriend come to see him, as well as my older sister's son (my nephew), his sister (my niece), and her fiancé came to visit. They were going to get married in October, and my dad still wanted to be around so he could go.

My sister could not stay the whole summer because she had to return to work, so we had to figure out other arrangements. I decided that I was going to take a leave of absence from work. It is what is known as an FMLA (Family Medical Leave Act) leave. I could take time off from work for a period of time and my job would be safe. Though I would not get my full paycheck, I would get something.

So after a long month of my sister taking care of my dad, which I am sure she could write an entire book about, the reigns were then handed to me. She trained me in everything

I needed to know about being his primary caretaker. On July 25 my sister went back to Georgia. I could not have been more appreciative of her for making such a sacrifice in her life and for her help in taking such good care of my dad.

It was not an easy job taking care of my dad. He was very demanding at times, and I had to answer every beck and call that he had. I joked with him that all he lacked was a bell or a bullhorn to get me when I was needed. I had to get used to his schedule now. There was no more waking up at 4:00 a.m. to read. They were some long days, and we bonded in ways no one except maybe my older sister could ever imagine, but it was awesome.

I hesitantly took him to the casino when he wanted, went to 7-Eleven to pick up his scratch-off lottery tickets, which was quite a process for him to do. I have never seen anyone take so much time scratching off a ticket! It would take him sometimes a half hour with his precise method.

I really enjoyed the company of his hospice aide, and I could really see how she and my dad hit it off because she was just so loving, caring, and had a great sense of humor. You have to be a special person to be able to put up with my dad.

He talked about wanting to go to a bay to watch ships come in at sea. I told him that the closest place we could do that was in Philadelphia, but he said he didn't want to go.

We had some really good conversations, bonding moments, and special times during this time together. It was actually nice to talk with him about the faith, because he was in the faith, so it was quite a transition.

He had some moments where he would get deeply depressed. And although some of the time it was because he still had a fear of dying, other times were because he really felt guilty about the past sins he had committed in his life.

It was truly a blessing to see my role with him change as I went from a Christian to an apologist to an evangelist, and now to pastoral caretaker. The main thing that I told him was that there was no need to feel guilty anymore, he had been forgiven, and now he had the righteousness of Christ. I knew that it was a hard concept to grasp, but it was true, and it was all because of God's love, mercy, and grace. God did not see him for who he was, God saw him for who he is in Jesus. The most important thing he needed to remember was that the Bible says in Romans 8:1: "There is therefore now no condemnation to them which are in Christ Jesus, who walk not after the flesh, but after the Spirit."

God has declared us not guilty because we put our faith in Jesus. We are free, so there was no need to feel this way anymore. His sins have been wiped out.

He began to ask honest questions, and it was awesome to see him search, seek, and finally realize how powerful the Christian faith really was.

The problem was that I rarely saw my wife or kids. I missed them very much. I mean, they would stop downstairs from time to time. Though we lived in the same house, I was always downstairs and they were upstairs, so I knew it was putting a strain on all of them. We did get to spend some quality time together here and there, and I think that the entire experience of my wife and I not being together actually made us appreciate our marriage more.

My wife and I had a conversation in our kitchen while my sister flew up from Georgia to give me some relief on a weekend and took care of my dad. I said to her that I thought that Dad was going to die soon. I just had that feeling. She said that she did not want to make things worse, but I always said that God was in control, and then she put on the counter two pregnancy tests that were positive. What a summer, and I was glad to share the joy with my dad while he was still alive.

I think that my dad could sense that his time was drawing near because he started to dispense all his jewelry and things to his kids. The one thing he did not keep in mind was that he loved to wear rings, and now that they were gone, he said that he felt naked.

He asked me if I had any that he could borrow, and I let him wear the Marine Corps ring that he got me when I graduated boot camp.

He put it on and it fit. He looked at it and said, "I like this ring. I want to be buried in it."

I said, "Dad, do you know where that ring came from? You got it for me when I graduated boot camp! It means the world to me!"

He said, "So what? Get another one."

This was him; he truly was a piece of work.

As time went on, his condition began to get worse. He was more off balance, needed a roll cart to walk, and he started to withdraw himself from things that he enjoyed to do.

He did not want to go to the casino anymore, current news did not interest him, he stopped smoking cigarettes, stopped getting up to use the bathroom, and all he wanted to do was sleep. This basically was part of the dying process, and though very hard to watch, we just had to come to terms that death was approaching.

He then became incoherent and would just lie in his hospice bed. The nurse said that he would probably be gone soon. The nurse's aide changed his clothes, washed him in bed, and did what she needed to do to keep him comfortable.

He was not eating anymore, and I began to administer pain medication orally by squirting it into his mouth. I also had to open the inevitable plastic bag given to us by hospice and started to use the blue square sponge on a white stick to dip into a glass of water with ice cubes and run it along his lips and in his mouth in hope of some type of relief for him.

This was quite a depressing turn of events for me. Just days ago I was serving him a cool glass of ice cubes and iced tea and he could drink it himself, enjoy the taste, and now there I was holding a stick and putting a damp sponge in my dad's mouth.

Besides me talking to him, with no responses, that was the only expression of kindness and compassion that I could offer to him as not only his caregiver, but as his son.

With every dip into the glass with the stick, as the wet, cool sponge soaked his mouth and lips, I could only hope that it would be sufficient enough to give him one last burst of strength to say one last word to me, but it never happened.

As the reoccurring scene happened over and over again, it reminded me of Jesus's last moments on the cross. In all four Gospels the event is recorded as such:

And straightway one of them ran, and took a spunge, and filled it with vinegar, and put it on a reed, and gave him to drink. (Matthew 27:48)

And one ran and filled a spunge full of vinegar, and put it on a reed, and gave him to drink, saying, Let alone; let us see whether Elias will come to take him down. (Mark 15:36)

And the soldiers also mocked him, coming to him, and offering him vinegar. (Luke 23:36)

Now there was set a vessel full of vinegar: and they filled a spunge with vinegar, and put it upon hyssop, and put it to his mouth. (John 19:29)

This fulfilled the long-awaited prophecy, written hundreds of years before Jesus's ministry, which states, "And in my thirst they gave me vinegar to drink" (Psalm 69:21).

Which Jesus knew, as He states in John 19:28, "After this, Jesus knowing that all things were now accomplished, that the scripture might be fulfilled, saith, I thirst."

As John records, "Now there was set a vessel full of vinegar," this may have been a jar of sour wine that could have been a thirst quencher similar to our Gatorade intended for the Roman soldiers to keep them hydrated while they fulfilled their physical obligations of crucifixion. Or perhaps it was just vinegar as Matthew, Mark, and Luke record a, "filled spunge full of vinegar." Was this an act of compassion for Jesus to quench His thirst or were some of the bystanders hoping to see the old superstition of Elijah appearing to help someone who was suffering and in great need? Could the vinegar offered to Jesus meant to have been to speed up his death with cheap wine that turned into vinegar with no desire to relieve Jesus' suffering? Could it have been an act as only a cruel intention to prolong death by reviving Jesus? Bible commentaries differ on their views, but it was a depressing image in my mind as I used a sponge for my dad as an act of compassion to help him.

Whether my dad was thirsty or not, this was all I could do anymore. I did know that though he was dying physically, spiritually he had all that he needed for his hunger and thirst: "And Jesus said unto them, I am the bread of life: he that cometh to me shall never hunger; and he that believeth on me shall never thirst" (John 6:35).

This is what kept me going through those tough times.

I called my sister in Georgia, and she took the next available flight out. I called my two younger sisters, and we spent as much time with him as we could, talking to him and holding his hand.

It was a very sad time for us, but we all have to come to terms with the fact that death is a part life.

CHAPTER 15

Going Home

On the morning of September 11, 2015, with all three of my sisters, my mother, and his hospice nurse's aide standing around him, holding his hands, whispering words of comfort, with tears in all of our eyes, we watched my dad take his final breath at 10:47 a.m. with "On the Dock of the Bay" by Otis Redding on the television radio station in the background.

It seemed fitting, for this is what he told me he wanted to do—sit on a dock of a bay and watch ships come in. It was pretty amazing to think that some of the song lyrics go, "Sittin' in the morning sun, I'll be sittin' when the evening comes. Watching the ships roll in. Then I watch them roll away again, yeah. I'm sittin' on the dock of the bay. Watchin' the tide roll away, ooh. I'm just sittin' on the dock of the bay, Wastin' time. Sittin' here resting my bones."

He was finally at rest and no doubt resting his bones.

We all held hands around him and said the Lord's Prayer together. I think the most important part of that prayer for me at that given moment was, "Thy will be done." We knew it was coming, and now was the time.

The next couple of hours felt like a bad dream. I'll tell you there is nothing more eerie than to see the funeral parlor employees come, put your own father in a black body bag, zip it up, carry him out, put him on a gurney, and take him to the hearse.

I was upset that he was gone, but I had joy in my heart knowing where his spirit was. It gave me great comfort to know that I would see him again someday. I just did not know how people who were not in the faith were able to cope, grieve, and mourn for someone that has died without having faith and hope in seeing that person again someday. It really made me wonder and deeply strengthened my faith.

As time went on, I had to get a sermon ready for his funeral. I thought no better place to write it than at his computer, listening to oldies in the background, and drinking his favorite liquor Grand Marnier, so I did just that. I poured myself a snifter and then went to town writing a sermon.

I was holding up pretty well until the day before the funeral. I decided to go for a drive to clear my head, but I just could not do it. I had the sermon with me, and I knew that I had to practice, so what I decided to do was go to where he was going to be buried. His plot was right next to his father and stepmother, my Gummy and Poppy.

I pulled into the cemetery, and as I got closer to his grave, I noticed that the grave was dug. There were wooden boards over it so no one would fall into it.

I got out of my car, grabbed the sermon, and walked over to his grave. It was very humbling to know that the following day his body would be inside of a coffin, put inside the hole, and his physical body would finally be laid to rest.

It was a pretty clear day. It was not too hot, but not too cool, just perfect, and there was no wind or breeze at all. The air was perfectly still, and the sun was shining bright. I stood before the empty grave in front of me and preached my sermon.

At the end, I began to cry. I also started to doubt if I could really do this tomorrow. I mean, could I really preach at my dad's funeral? Was everything that I believed true? I needed and prayed for some type of comfort, peace, and assurance at that very moment.

I never in my entire walk as a Christian had any doubts up until then. All of a sudden, the stillness of the air broke and there was a cool breeze. It hit my face, and I felt a peace that I never felt before. The words, "Believe what you are saying, because it is true," kept running through my heart, mind, and soul.

But what was I saying? I just said my sermon, and the primary focal point was that my dad was at rest, he was only asleep, and that I would see him again one day.

At that moment, I felt comfort and peace like I had never felt before, and all of my doubt was lifted! It was truly amazing. It made me think of 2 Corinthians 1:4, where it says, "Who comforteth us in all our tribulation, that we may be able to comfort them which are in any trouble, by the comfort wherewith we ourselves are comforted of God." I also thought of Philippians 4:7, where it says, "And the peace of God, which passeth all understanding, shall keep your hearts and minds through Christ Jesus."

The funeral the next day went very well. Each one of my sisters spoke or did a reading during the service. We even had a friend of the family who knew my dad well sing "Amazing Grace."

Many people showed up, which was awesome to see. I kept hearing that the words that I said gave closure to some people, and they said that this is the way a funeral should be. Some could not understand how I could give the sermon at my own dad's funeral. The simple answer was because he was only sleeping, and I would see him again someday.

That part of the service was now over, and the doors were closed. Me and close family said our final good-byes with the casket open. We all took a good look at him. He was wearing one of his favorite hats, a pair of glasses, and a shirt that he loved very much. In the outside pocket of his shirt, we put a winning lottery ticket that he scratched but never cashed. It was not a big win, but he went out a winner. The final item that I looked at was my Marine Corps ring on his finger. His hands were folded on his chest, and the ring gleamed in the lights.

The casket then was closed. An American flag was draped over top of the casket, and the other pallbearers and I carried him out to the hearse that was going to take him to the cemetery.

I sat in the passenger seat of the hearse and took my final ride with my dad. When we pulled up to the cemetery I saw two Marines in dress blues. One was a little ways from the graveside playing taps on his bugle, and the other one was standing at attention near the grave.

What I needed to do was talk to them to see if instead of handing the flag to someone, they could just lay it on the casket. This is what my sisters and I decided would be best to do, so it would avoid confusion and taking the honor of someone personally getting the flag handed to them.

I got out of the hearse, and the funeral director walked over with me to one of the Marines. I told him that I was the son of the deceased, and I actually was the chaplain who was saying the last part of the service. He asked me to give him a signal to let him know when I was done speaking so they could start the folding of the flag tribute. We worked that out and then I asked him if instead of handing the flag to someone he could just place it on top of the casket. He said that he could not.

In all actuality, I understood why, but I did not know what to do. The funeral director was already over talking to my sisters. He then came running back and said to the Marine, "I just spoke with his sisters. I told them that you could not place the flag on the casket and that you had to hand the flag to someone. They all voted unanimously that you should hand it to the deceased's son."

My heart nearly stopped. I was just so humbled.

I walked back to the hearse. The pallbearers took hold of the coffin, I walked out in front about ten feet of it, and then I led the way to the grave.

The casket was placed on the boards above the grave, and I said the last part of my service. I gave the Marine a nod, and the two Marines started the flag-folding process. It was like time had stopped. I could not believe it was all over.

The flag was then finally and perfectly folded. The Marine carrying it walked over, stood directly in front of me, and said, "This flag is presented to you on behalf of the president of the United States, the United States Marine Corps, and a grateful nation in memory of the years of dedication and faithful service of your father. May God bless you and thank you."

I could not help but shed some tears standing there holding that flag. I put my hand on the casket and said in my mind, *Rest in peace, big guy, my best friend, my dad. I never have lived a day without you, so going forward is not going to be easy. But I thank God for His hope in Christ that we will see each other again someday. I do not say good-bye, but only until we see each other again. Enjoy your nap. I know how you like your naps.*

The funeral was finally over, and everyone was invited to a restaurant down the road for a lunch in memory of my dad. A long time ago my dad had purchased the biggest bottle of Grand Marnier on the market. He told us that he wanted it opened at his funeral and for everyone to have a drink. His request was honorably granted as we all took part and actually finished the bottle. The waitress poured the last of what was left in the bottle and said that my dad would have probably wanted it to go to me. I drank it with pieces of cork and all, but I was still humbled.

Now that my dad was gone, it was time to go back to work and try to get back to normal. Though I missed him dearly, I knew he finally was at peace, and it was time to get back into the swing of things.

It is a funny thing when someone close to you dies because most people who know you want to offer words of comfort. The problem is that sometimes they just don't know what to say, say the wrong things altogether, or even just try to avoid you. It can make for a very uncomfortable experience for both the comforter and the person being comforted.

A lot of the times when you hear things people say to try and offer comfort you think to yourself that it probably would have been better if they had just not said anything.

If you are a Bible-believing Christian such as I am, you know the word pretty well. So when I heard people say to me in the weeks after my dad's death things like I have listed below, it just made me walk away knowing that I was happy to have a relationship with God, know His word, and His promises. He truly is the only source of comfort I could rely on.

The below are some actual conversations I had.

Christian comforter: "I am so sorry for your loss, but your dad is now an angel in heaven."

What I wanted to say was: "Thank you, but he is not an angel. An angel is a separate being, and humans do not become angels when they die. Jesus said we will be 'like' angels, but we will not become one. Do you read your Bible?"

What I actually said was: "Thank you for offering your words of encouragement."

Christian comforter: "It's okay, your dad is your guardian angel now."

What I wanted to say was: "Thank you, but he is not an angel. An angel is a separate being, and humans do not become angels when they die. Jesus said we will be 'like' angels, but we will not become one. I was also more than likely assigned an angel the moment I accepted Christ as my Lord and Savior; this is what the book of Hebrews hints at. This happened in 2008 for me. My dad was actually an agnostic then and was living a life far away from Jesus. Do you read your Bible?"

What I actually said was:

"Thank you for offering your words of encouragement."

Christian comforter: "It's okay, your dad is in heaven now."

What I wanted to say was: "No, he is not. I don't quite think that you understand heaven and the Christian hope with resurrection. At the time of my dad's death, his soul left his physical body and went to some type of conscious disembodied state. He is with Christ, as Paul describes, which is far better than being alive, but not as close as being in glory as to our resurrection body. My dad's physical body is lying in his grave awaiting Christ's second coming, where Jesus will bring his soul back, as well as all other Christians who died in Christ. My dad's soul will then reunite with his physical body and receive a glorified resurrection body. He then will stand before the judgment seat of Christ and be placed into the new heavens and new earth with all other Christians. This is my understanding. Where do you get your understanding? Do you read your Bible?"

What I actually said was: "Thank you for offering your words of encouragement."

Christian comforter: "Your dad has his wings now."

What I wanted to say was:

"My dad did not drink Red Bull, so I'm not sure what you are implying. Do you mean he is like transformed into a bird or an angel or something? I don't quite understand why you said that. It really does not make any sense. Do you read your Bible?

What I actually said was: "Thank you for offering your words of encouragement."

Christian comforter: "You will get over this, it will just take time."

What I wanted to say was: "No. I probably will not. No one really gets over missing someone who has died. In time I will more than likely just learn to live with the pain. But I do have God's promise that I will see him again someday. This is what keeps me going. Do you read your Bible?"

What I actually said was: "Thank you for offering your words of encouragement."

Christian comforter: "Everything is going to be all right."

What I wanted to say was: "Really? How so? Please give me some examples. My dad is dead, I am deeply saddened, I am grieving, mourning, and I miss him dearly. He was my father and best friend. How could you say such a thing? Do you read your Bible?"

What I actually said was: "Thank you for offering your words of encouragement."

Non-Christian comforter: "I am sure your dad will be reincarnated and come back as a really great person, as he once was."

What I wanted to say was: "The Bible says that we are appointed to die just once. Not over and over again. We only get one chance in life, and we need Jesus because He is the only way to salvation. My dad accepted this fact before he died, and he is now with Him. Obviously you are not Christian. Let's talk."

What I actually said was: "The Bible says that we are appointed to die just once. Not over and over again. We only get one chance in life and we need Jesus because He is the only way to salvation. My dad accepted that fact before he died, and he is now with him. Obviously you are not Christian. Let's talk."

I heard many supposed words of comfort, but I have come to realize that the thing we must understand is that sometimes the best thing to say to someone who is mourning the loss of someone is just not to say anything at all.

A hand on the shoulder, maybe even a hug, or just simple words like, "My condolences," go a long way. We can learn a lot from Job's friends as I talked about earlier. The wisest thing that Job's three friends did was sit with him for seven days and seven nights without saying a word. It was only when they were trying to offer comfort and opened their mouths that they completely blew it. This is what made Job say, "I have heard many such things: miserable comforters are ye all" (Job 16:2).

No one wants to be a miserable comforter, especially when they think they are offering wise counsel like the examples I gave earlier. The worst part is with unwise words, the person in mourning becomes miserable themselves and is not comforted whatsoever.

We must learn to choose our words wisely, whether or not others do so, and we must lead by example if we are to be true ambassadors for Christ.

CHAPTER 16

Finale

In this book I have shared with you my testimony. I hoped to accomplish a few things in doing so. If you are a Christian, I hope that my testimony and these words have encouraged you. Your faith is not in vain. If you feel ill-equipped to defend what you believe, there is a lot of help out there. You may be a blue-collar believer and think that you may not have the time to commit to researching troubling questions that you may have or others might potentially ask you, research other religions, or even just have a fear of defending your faith. In all honestly, you do not need a lot of time. Reading and studying here and there can go a long way. There are very helpful books, as well as awesome apologetics ministries you can look into. Talk to an elder at your church about starting an apologetics study at your church once a week similar to a Bible study. If you do not think that it is important to be able to defend what you believe, you are wrong.

> But sanctify the Lord God in your hearts: and be ready always to give an answer to every man that

> asketh you a reason of the hope that is in you with meekness and fear: Having a good conscience; that, whereas they speak evil of you, as of evildoers, they may be ashamed that falsely accuse your good conversation in Christ. (1 Peter 3:15–16)

Keep this verse in mind because there is so much truth to it. I really feel that we must know what is going on in the world around us, and the only way to defend the faith properly is to have an understanding of what other people believe.

We live in a world where you can believe just about anything, but that does not make it true. People cannot just say, "What is true for you is not true for me."

This is a fallacy known as a relativist or subjective fallacy. For example, if I believe two plus two is three, and you believe two plus two is four, obviously I am wrong. Believe it or not, the same principle applies for your eternal destination. There is either a life after death or there is not; they cannot be both correct. There are also people that think all religions are basically the same and lead us to God. Jesus diminishes that assertion when He says in John 14:6, "I am the way, the truth, and the life: no man cometh unto the Father, but by Me."

Clearly from Jesus's words above all religions are not basically the same and lead to God. Either Jesus was right or He was wrong; it cannot be both ways. What it all boils down to is His resurrection. Either He rose from the grave or He did not. Paul knew this when he said that if Christ did not rise from the dead, then the Christian faith is worthless.

From the early days of Christianity, as I discussed earlier on in this book, when I expounded on some elements in a discussion with my dad I debunked supposed theories that explain away the resurrection.

The bottom line is that either the resurrection happened or it did not. Over two thousand years later, Jesus's body has still not been found. Seems to me, as well as all Christians, that what Jesus said is true: "I am the resurrection, and the life: he that believeth in Me, though he were dead, yet shall he live" (John 11:25).

It also says in Mark 8:31, "And He began to teach them, that the Son of man must suffer many things, and be rejected of the elders, and of the chief priests, and scribes, and be killed, and after three days rise again."

This is the difference between Christianity and all other religions. Jesus's tomb is empty, and every other founder of any other religion's tomb is still occupied. Take for example the claims of the Quran. Yet again, it all boils down to whether or not Jesus rose from the dead.

Christianity says He did.

Islam says that He didn't.

In the words of Paul, it seemed he was given divine revelation about what was going to happen six hundred years later when the angel spoke to Muhammed and told him that Jesus did not die at the crucifixion when he penned the words in Galatians 1:8: "But though we, or an angel from heaven, preach any other gospel unto you than that which we have preached unto you, let him be accursed."

Who do we believe here?

Paul or Muhammad?

People who walked, talked, and saw with their own eyes Jesus's life, death, and resurrection, or someone who claims to have been visited by an angel that comes along six hundred years later stating that Paul and the disciples got it all wrong?

The same can be said about any other religion in the world. If you do the research, you will come to find that Jesus is the only one who claimed to conquer death and all of those who believe in Him will have eternal life.

Paul was familiar with what was going on in the world around him and what people believed. He even quoted in the New Testament non-Christian poets and philosophers to point to the gospel in Acts 17:28: "'For in him we live and move and have our being.' As some of your own poets have said, 'We are his offspring.'"

He was most likely referring to the Greek poet Aratus.

In Titus 1:12 it reads, "One of Crete's own prophets has said it: 'Cretans are always liars, evil brutes, lazy gluttons.'"

He was most likely referring to the Cretan philosopher Epimenides.

Elsewhere he may in fact have quoted the Greek poet Menander. The bottom line is that Paul is a perfect example of a Christian having an idea of the basic beliefs of people and then pointing them to the gospel.

If you are a non-Christian and are an honest seeker, I do hope that what you have read has helped you in your search. Jesus is the answer to all of life's biggest and toughest questions. There are answers; you just have to take the time to look with an open mind and heart. In Matthew 7:7–8, Jesus said, "Ask, and it shall be given you; seek, and ye shall find; knock, and it shall be opened unto you: For every one that asketh receiveth; and he that seeketh findeth; and to him that knocketh it shall be opened."

Wise words—please do take them into consideration.

In conclusion, I just want to share one final thought. Before my dad died, I never would have thought I would be able to live a day without him. I mean, I never actually did. When he became a Christian though, I knew that his salvation was secure, and I could go on the rest of my mortal life without him because I just know in my heart that I will see him again.

Before I had children, I was scared to death to have any. When my wife and I were expecting our first child, our daughter, I honestly said to myself, *How am I going to be a father? I am not going to be able to do this!* When I had my second child, my son, I had the same thoughts. Now with my third child on the way I don't think these things anymore. There was a time in my life when I couldn't imagine being a father and having children, but now that they are here, I cannot imagine my life without them.

This same principle goes for Jesus in my life. I lived many years without Him, but now I cannot imagine a day without Him. He has changed my life so much. He can and will do the same for you, if you just believe.

For God so loved the world, that he gave his only begotten Son, that whosoever believeth in him should not perish, but have everlasting life.—John 3:16

That if thou shalt confess with thy mouth the Lord Jesus, and shalt believe in thine heart that God hath raised him from the dead, thou shalt be saved.—Romans 10:9

Take the step now. He is waiting.

If you do, I hope to meet you someday, and you can tell me how this book as touched you. If not in this life then certainly in the next.

ABOUT THE AUTHOR

Chaplain Bill's voice is unparalleled. Though most Christian authors share long lists of academic credentials, his would be among the shortest, as scholarly degrees are not a part of his outline. What clearly makes his writing distinctive is that his audience noticeably senses his divine duty to write and recognizes the "something special" that stands out within his words. Though he has obtained various specialized academic certificates, his main credentials are from his life experiences, which cannot be earned in a classroom setting, but only through intimate personal encounters. When getting to know him through Blue Collar Believer, the reader soon discovers that he has a charismatic personality, which he feels is absolutely guided by the Holy Spirit. Readers will be pleasantly surprised that someone who was called into the ministry in his thirties is truly doing the Lord's will, and lack of education is not a hindrance in using his talents and spiritual gifts as an Ambassador of Christ. He hopes to inspire others to do the same; when all they hear is the world saying "No," God, CAN and WILL use that someone and say ""Yes"."

Printed in the United States
By Bookmasters